"Bill Pistrui has written a biography of his father, Traian, who immigrated to the United States in 1909 at age nine. He lived in the St. Louis, Missouri area until his death at age 104. Traian Pistrui was born in Beba Veche, a small farming village at the westernmost point of Romania, just a few miles from the present-day borders of Hungary and Serbia.

The book is a record of Traian's life as told to his son, including incidents of his childhood in Romania (then Hungary), his trip to America on the SS Carpathia, and his assimilation into a predominantly Irish community in St. Louis area. It also includes details of Traian's adult life from marriage to work life to retirement. Mr. Pistrui conducted research to flesh out the story of his father's Ellis Island experience, and he relays his "mother's perceived arranged marriage to my father," quoting her as saying, "Your daddy captured me, put shoes on me and dragged me to the altar."

Mr. Pistrui's *The Immigrant* is based on a true story of family values, hard work, accepting responsibilities and fulfillment. It is the story of one of millions of emigrants who came to America from Eastern Europe and made America great while still proudly embracing their heritage."

—*Vicki Albu*, *President, Romanian Genealogy Society*

The Immigrant

iUniverse books may be ordered through booksellers or by contacting:

iUniverse
1663 Liberty Drive
Bloomington, IN 47403
www.iuniverse.com
1-800-Authors (1-800-288-4677)

Because of the dynamic nature of the internet, any any web addresses or links contained in this book may have changed since publication and may no longer be valid. The views expressed in this work are solely those of the author and do not necessarily reflect the views of the publisher, and the publisher hereby disclaims any responsibility for them.

Any people depicted in stock imagery provided by Getty Images are models, and such images are being used for illustrative purposes only. Certain stock imagery © Getty Images.

ISBN: 978-1-5320-9268-8 (sc)
ISBN: 978-1-5320-9269-5 (hc)
ISBN: 978-1-5320-9267-1 (e)

Library of Congress Control Number: 2020902250

Print information available on the last page.

iUniverse rev. date: 07/31/2020

This book is dedicated to my lovely wife, Nonie, the vivacious young executive secretary who financially supported me during our first two years of marriage while I was still in college. After I graduated, she agreed to be a stay-at-home mom and made the necessary sacrifices so that we could live on only my income, which allowed me all the freedom and flexibility that I felt I needed to advance in my chosen profession. To Nonie, God's gift to me, I owe everything.

PREFACE

The Immigrant is a true story about my father, who immigrated to the United States in 1909 when he was nine years old. He lived in the St. Louis area up until the ripe old age of 104.

The book started as a record of Dad's life as he told it to me. Incidents of his childhood in Romania, the trip to America on the *Carpathia* (the ship that would rescue the *Titanic* several years later), and his assimilation into an Irish neighborhood in St. Louis are included in the narrative as best as I can remember. He never told me anything about Ellis Island. It never came up when he reminisced about his childhood.

The remainder of the biography was to be about the rest of Dad's life, with me as the narrator. When I got to the chapter on Ellis Island, I had nothing to go on from what Dad had told me, but I was interested in what vetting would have been like when Dad had come over.

I obtained a book entitled *The Illustrated Encyclopedia of Ellis Island* by Barry Moreno and started my research on what vetting was like when my father came to America in 1909. I allowed my imagination to create incidents involving his mother, aunt, and younger sister at Ellis Island, which could have happened. It was then that I decided to change the format of this book from the biography of my father to a historical novel that was based on a true story, with me as one of the many characters in the story.

The incidents involving my mother's perceived arranged marriage to my father came directly from my memories of her often talking about it when I was growing up. "Your daddy captured me, put shoes on me, and then dragged me to the altar," she would often say with a laugh when I asked about how she had met Dad.

The book ended up as some kind of a hybrid—neither beast nor fowl—with some aspects of biography, history, Romanian heritage, and a beautiful love story. It is my hope that it will be of interest to the many Romanian families in America who can identify with some of the incidents in the book.

For those less fortunate (not blessed with Romanian heritage), it is my hope that they will enjoy reading the following story as much as I enjoyed writing it.

TABLE OF CONTENTS

CHAPTER 1
PEASANT LIFE

It was harvest time in Beba Veche, a small village in Austria-Hungary. The year was 1902. The ripened wheat was being cut by hand. The blades of the scythes had been sharpened the night before by each man with the slow, careful strokes of a handheld sharpening stone. A row of about two dozen men with razor-sharp scythes made sweeping arcs several inches above the ground. Behind each man was a woman who raked the cut wheat and bound it with twine into bundles, which would be counted at the end of the day. Each man-and-woman team was paid for the number of wheat bundles that they produced.

The land that was being harvested was managed by a local representative of the landowner, who was never seen. The head of each family in Beba Veche had made an agreement with the manager to plant and harvest the field for a given amount of money. The agreement was renewed each year. To keep the peasants in line, the landowner would occasionally not renew the agreement and choose not to plant the village field. This left the peasants facing a year of hunger as they had to eke out nourishment from their own small garden plots and butcher their prize lambs and goats, which were being saved for breeding.

Since the landowner had fields in adjacent villages, the revenue he lost from one uncultivated field had little effect on his standard of living. Meanwhile, peasants in adjacent villages would also get the message to keep in line.

———◆———

Ioan and his wife, Johanna, waited while the manager recorded the number of bundles that they had produced. They were the first people in the field at sunrise and the last to quit as the sun set. Drenched in perspiration, they smiled at each other as the manager gave them his count and told them that they had more bundles of wheat than any other couple did. This was common for them.

Ioan was twenty-nine years old, five feet, six inches tall, and highly energetic. His wife, Johanna, who was five years younger and several inches shorter than he was, had acquired the reputation of being the strongest woman in Beba Veche. Many even said that she was as strong as some men were.

Together they walked to a wagon, which was shading their two-and-a-half-year-old son, Traian, who had been taken to the field with them that morning, while Traian's six-month-old sister, Flora, was being cared for in the village by Ioan's mother. Johanna picked up the sleeping

Traian, wrapped him in his blanket, and handed him to her husband. Then she climbed up and seated herself in the cart. After handing Traian back to his wife, Ioan got into the cart, grabbed the reins, and urged the horse forward.

Johanna noticed that Traian was sleeping more soundly than usual. She lifted him up close to her face and smelled liquor on his breath. Traian had helped himself to the flask of liquor that Ioan had stowed under the wagon with their lunch.

The twenty-three-year-old mother seemed more bothered than concerned about Traian's condition. She had Ioan stop at the public watering trough when they arrived in the village of Beba Veche. Ioan held Traian while Johanna climbed down from the cart. Then she reached up for the sleeping Traian. After immersing him completely in water, she handed him to Ioan, and climbed back into the cart.

In those days, peasant life in Beba Veche was similar to the medieval feudal system where a large landowner would give a family a small plot of ground in return for the family being allowed to plant and harvest a larger segment of adjacent land, which was owned by the landowner. On the small plot of ground, the peasant family would build a house, plant a vegetable garden, and raise livestock, which usually consisted of two horses, a cow, several sheep and goats, and a few chickens.

Ioan, the oldest son of Ioan-Stephan, lived with his father and mother on a plot of ground that dated back to Ioan's great-grandfather, who was born in Beba Veche in 1804. Their house was on about an acre of land at the edge of the village. The front half of the house had two rooms, which were separated by a wall of the fireplace. The room was sixteen feet wide and twelve feet deep, with the fireplace centered along a wall. To the right of the fireplace, there was a masonry baking oven. To the left, there was a door to the bedroom, which belonged to Ioan's parents. Heat radiated from the back wall of the masonry fireplace and provided heat for the bedroom.

In the entry room, there was a large table used for both food preparation and dining. Along the walls, there were two beds and a crib, which were used by Ioan, his wife, and his two children. Above this area was an attic, which was accessed by a ladder. This area would be used as a bedroom by Traian when he got old enough to climb the ladder.

The inside of the house was quite colorful. Several framed religious icons, hand-embroidered leather waistcoats, and leather belts for weddings and other special celebrations hung on the white walls. One bedspread had pink and red flowers embroidered on a white cotton background. The other bed was covered with a knitted wool blanket. It had broad stripes of red, green, and white, which had been knitted by Johanna when she was a teenager.

Across the rear of the house and along its full twenty-eight-foot length, a twelve-foot-deep lean-to had been added, which sheltered the livestock. The exterior walls of the house were made of mud, which had been reinforced with straw and set in wood forms. As the mud had dried, the forms had been moved up in twelve-inch lifts until the wall was eight feet high.

Across the ceiling, there were exposed wood beams and planks that served as the attic floor. The steep sloped roof was made of wood rafters and small beams, which had been closely spaced to accommodate a thatched roof. Both the outside and inside of the adobe walls had been painted white with a slurry made of powdered lime and water. The houses had been constructed entirely by the relatives, who had worked together in teams.

As Ioan stopped the wagon in front of his house, he was greeted by his mother, Elena, who took Traian from Johanna's arms.

"Why is he so wet?" asked Elena.

After being told the story by Johanna, Elena said with a laugh, "Getting drunk at his age is a bad start for him."

Ioan's father took the horse and wagon to the rear of the house where he unharnessed the horse and led it to a manger with hay while Ioan and Johanna went to the well to get a drink and to freshen up with splashes of cold well water across their faces.

Although it was a part of Austria-Hungary, the village of Beba Veche consisted mostly of peasants who were Romanians. It was within the region known as Banat, which lay to the southwest of Transylvania. In 1902, both Banat and Transylvania were part of Austria-Hungary. However, nearly all the people in these two regions spoke Romanian and were descendants of the Roman soldiers who had conquered the area, which had been known as Dacia, around AD 106, under the Roman emperor Trajan. The Romans had intermarried with the Dacians, who had adopted Roman customs and the Latin language. All local public officials in Beba Veche, along with police and school teachers, were Hungarians.

The evening meal consisted of hot cornmeal mush (*mamaliga*), homemade goat cheese, and bread with butter. On Mondays and Thursdays, Elena baked two loaves of bread. On Tuesdays and Fridays, she churned butter and made cheese. Dairy products needed to be consumed quickly before they spoiled.

Meat, when available, was eaten on Thursdays and Sundays. Ham, bacon, and sausage, which were stored in the smokehouse from the previous fall's butchering, supplemented Sunday's freshly killed chickens. On special holidays, fresh meat, which came from pigs, lambs, and goats that were butchered early in the morning, was cooked and eaten the same day by family members.

On the side of their house and opposite the animals' shelter, there was a vegetable garden. At the edge of the village, two acres of land had been assigned to Ioan's family by the landowner. When they were not working in the landowner's field, Ioan's family members planted and harvested these two acres, which provided food and additional money for the family. This would be added to the money that had been earned from harvesting the landowner's field.

Even with all these resources, quantities of food and money were still sparse for the family, and disciplined management was necessary for bare subsistence. Nothing was wasted.

After their prayer before the evening meal, which had been prepared by Ioan's mother, Ioan's father said, "We have a new school teacher."

"Oh," said Ioan. "What was wrong with Attila? I kind of liked him. He was a good teacher and kind to the children."

Ioan's father replied, "From what I hear, that was the problem. He was too kind."

"Have you met the new one?" asked Ioan.

"No, but I hear that the Romanian language and grammar will no longer be taught and all of our children must learn Hungarian."

"I don't like that," Ioan said with a frown.

After they finished their evening meal, Ioan replaced a broken wooden peg in Johanna's rake, which she would use in the field. Following that, he took out his sharpening stone and began stroking the blade of his scythe while his father took food scraps out to the newly born pigs. While all this was happening, Johanna was mending the rip in Ioan's only pair of field trousers.

Johanna looked forward to weddings in Beba Veche. This was a time when she would transform herself from a perspiring field hand and struggling mother of two infant children into a person of dignity. The soiled, patched garments of a typical day would be replaced by a white linen blouse, which had embroidery on it, and a skirt. She would cover this with a bright half-apron, which had a red-and-white-striped pattern on it.

She had made all these things herself before she had been married. She had bought her shiny black shoes from the village cobbler when she was seventeen and had hidden them in a special box, which she had placed under her bed.

Weddings were special events for Johanna. She also looked forward to Orthodox mass because of its elaborate ceremony. The wedding's sounds of music and hymns, the smell of candle wax and incense, the prayers of the Orthodox priest, and the vows of the happy couple gave her a feeling of being in another world.

After the service, a celebration followed. A line of women in the embroidered costumes faced a line of men in tight woven trousers, calf-high boots, and embroidered leather waistcoats over long-sleeved white blouses. Each person in line had his or her arms locked around the waists of the next person and made skipping steps to one side and then to the other.

Following that, all who were in the line unlocked their arms, which allowed the men and women to skip toward each other, lock arms, and dance around a circle together while the observers clapped in unison. The crowning touch to the celebration was the bits of roast lamb and pastries to eat and toasts to the bride and groom, which were made with homemade wine and liquor.

These were the occasions when Johanna found herself in a different world. She had no aching muscles, no wheat to bind, no goats to milk, but only music and laughter. The only other form of recreation Johanna had was the street dance in Beba Veche's village square. These were held on Saturdays, weather permitting, with music provided by a local group of gypsies. The music came from violins, flutes, concertinas, and tambourines. Placed in front of the musicians was a small bowl for coins. Next to it was a small basket for fruit and vegetables from dancers who had no coins to spare for the musicians.

For these occasions, Johanna wore the clothes she had set aside for Sunday mass—one of the two changes of clothes she had for that purpose. The exception was her shoes. For these dances, Johanna wore her field shoes, which prevented damage to her nice pair. She wore the nice pair to mass on Sundays and weddings.

In 1904, when Traian was five years old, he was able to climb the ladder to his bed in the loft. This consisted of a straw-filled mattress, a pillow, and two quilts, which had been made by his grandmother Elena before she had married his grandfather Stephan. The bed was next to the chimney to take advantage of the heat that radiated from it in the winter.

By that time, his younger sister, Flora, was three years old and was moved from her cradle to Traian's bed to make room for the expected new baby. The baby was delivered with the assistance of Elena and the village midwife. The new baby was a boy. They named him Chiriac and placed him in the cradle that had been vacated by Flora.

Ioan's education took place in Beba Veche's small grammar school, where he became reasonably proficient in reading and writing Romanian, as well as simple arithmetic. Johanna never attended school. This was the custom for most peasant girls her age, who spent their youth learning to sew and cook from their illiterate mothers.

Even with his limited education, Ioan was able to acquire a part-time job for the local Hungarian government monitoring road improvements, which were performed by peasants when they were not working in the fields. His duties were to calculate and order the amount of gravel that was necessary to fill ruts in the road and to keep track of the time that the peasants spent distributing gravel on the road. For this, he was paid a very modest wage.

He saved this in a small leather-covered wooden chest in which he kept his other money. The chest was kept hidden in a niche in the wall, which was covered by a framed Orthodox icon of the Blessed Virgin Mary.

Like Johanna, Ioan was inspired by Orthodox religious practices, which gave him another world and relief from the aches of swinging a scythe under the midday sun. This is what his father had done. This is what his ancestors had done for generations. He was bound to and trapped by the land because of his lease with the representative of the Hungarian landowner. For Johanna, religion, weddings, and weekly dances were a time for relaxation and pleasure, from which she could draw strength to face and accept the world into which she had been born.

In the fall of 1905, Ioan introduced six-year-old Traian to his Hungarian schoolmaster on his first day there. Traian was frightened by the stern behavior of the schoolmaster and drew little comfort from his father's attempt to console him.

"Now, don't worry, Traian. Just do everything your teacher tells you to do, and everything will be all right," Ioan said.

Not everything was all right for Traian. The school consisted of one large room with about fifty children from ages six to thirteen. He did not know most of them.

His teacher's first remarks were, "Now, before we begin, I want you all to understand that you live in the country of Austria-Hungary. You are Hungarians and will learn the Hungarian language."

That evening, a confused and tearful Traian revealed the schoolmaster's opening remarks to his father. Ioan placed his hands on Traian's shoulders, looked him straight in the eye, and with deep compassion, softly but sternly said, "Your teacher was wrong. You are Romanian and will always be Romanian. As Romanians, we live under the rule of Austria-Hungary. Some day that may change, and we may live under the rule of a Romanian government. In the meantime, the best thing we can do is obey the Hungarians and hope that things will change."

Strengthened by his father's advice, Traian applied himself diligently to his studies. He learned to read and write Hungarian at school during the day and Romanian from his father at home in the evening. His Hungarian teacher was a strict taskmaster. Whenever he deemed one of his students needed corporal punishment, he gave the student a large knife and told him to cut a switch from the tree in the playground. If the switch was not thick enough, the teacher would cut one the size he considered appropriate. One evening, Traian told his father that the teacher lost patience with a girl student and yanked her ear, pulling her earring through its pierced earlobe.

About sixteen kilometers (ten miles) from the village of Beba Veche, there was a small town called Sânnicolau Mare. The town held a large fair in its square each fall, which Ioan made a point to attend. He and Johanna would leave Beba Veche early in the morning in their horse-drawn cart and return late in the evening with needed items that could not be purchased in Beba Veche. When Traian was six years old, he went with them. Johanna bought him a large cookie in the shape of a small sword. It was covered with icing and colored sugar. On that same trip, Ioan stopped at a booth manned by a Romanian agent. The agent represented one of several steamship lines that were competing for second- and third-class passengers emigrating from Europe to the United States.

Early in 1904, the Cunard Line and the Hungarian government had reached an agreement that would dramatically increase the number of third-class passengers going to America. Agents had been recruited to assist passengers with passports and other travel arrangements. The Cunard Line paid the Hungarian government forty kronen (eight dollars) for each person who immigrated to the United States.

"Hello," said the agent as Ioan walked into his booth, which had a table with maps to look at. "What can I do for you?"

"Tell me what you are offering," replied Ioan as he sat across the table from the agent.

"There is a need for workers in America. We have a Romanian contact in St. Louis who can help you get a job there."

"How much will I get paid?"

Ioan was amazed at the salary, which was five hundred kronen per year. Then he asked, "What would it cost me to live there?"

The agent laughed and said, "That depends on how well you want to live. Here is a list of prices for room rentals near the plant, along with the name and address of my contact in the small community of Romanians who are now living in St. Louis. He can verify what I am telling you." Although Ioan had little interest in going to the United States, he still took the information back to Beba Veche.

When Ioan finished the evening meal, he took out the information from the agent. He calculated how long it would take to save enough money, after going to America, to bring the rest of his family there. According to his calculations, it would take one year. This triggered his imagination. Could he live for a year without the warmth of Johanna's body next to his each night? How would Johanna, Traian, Flora, and Chiriac survive if the Hungarian landowner chose not to renew the harvesting lease?

Ioan still could not bring himself to face the uncertainties involving the welfare of his family. After folding up the agent's information, he decided to save it. As he took the small chest out of the niche, one of the papers he wanted to save fell from his fingers. As he picked it up, he noticed the name of the Romanian contact, followed by his street address in America. With a pensive shrug, Ioan decided to write a letter to this contact, which the agent had offered verification for, although he still was not enthusiastic about leaving Romania.

He wrote a simple one-page letter, included the information from the recruiter, and asked for a reply. The next day, Ioan gave the letter to Beba Veche's Hungarian postmaster, who stared at the address with a look of suspicion. "He's a distant relative, and I'm asking him for money," Ioan said in a casual manner.

After this, Ioan went back to his home to help his father plow their vegetable garden in preparation for the spring planting. Although he did not have high hopes for a response to his letter, his curiosity remained.

***

In the summer of 1906, Traian earned a few coins from his neighbors by taking their goats several days a week to graze on a grassy hill that was too steep for planting. Insisting that Traian save the coins, Ioan kept them in the chest, along with a slip of paper that kept track of the amounts and dates when Traian's coins were placed there.

On grazing days, Traian was given a large piece of bread, a chunk of raw bacon, and a small knife for cutting bite-size chunks. He ate this lunch in the shade of a large tree at the top of the slope. Since no water was available on the slope, Traian made sure he got his fill of the water from the last house's well before he reached the slope. The herd of twenty-four goats that he had collected from neighbors along the way accompanied him. On the way back in late afternoon, Traian again quenched his thirst at the house at the bottom of the slope.

"How many did you have today?" asked Ioan as Traian sat down for the evening meal.

"Twenty," said Traian.

"Why so few?"

"Several were about to have kids, and their owners wanted them close by."

After the evening meal, Ioan took a newspaper out from under his bed's mattress and began reading. It was a weekly publication called *Sămănătorul* (*The Sower*), which was written and published by a man named Nicolae Iorga. Nicolae lived in Iasi, a city located near the eastern border of Romania, about twenty miles from the border that separated Romania from Russia.

"If the Hungarian police learn that you are reading that paper, you will be put in jail," said Ioan's father as Ioan spread out the paper on the table near the window, which was lit by the late afternoon sun.

"Don't worry," said Ioan. "The only people that know I am reading this are you and the person who sold it to me, and I keep it well hidden."

Nicolae Iorga was a renowned educator, historian, and quasi politician. His mission was to unify all the Romanian-speaking people in Banat, Transylvania, and Romania into one country. He was a strong advocate for peasants and was deeply moved by their strong commitment to family, hard work, and religion.

He wanted their values to be at the core of the new Romania. He wanted peasants to have a voice in government. Although he was well respected as a historian, lecturer, and educator, his political views were not favored by the Romanian ruling class, who benefited from dominating the peasantry. As far as the Austria-Hungary government was concerned, he was a threat to its control of Banat and Transylvania.

Nicolae Iorga was Ioan's only hope for a better life. If Iorga's mission could be accomplished, life for Ioan's family would be more secure. They would no longer have to worry about renewing the land lease each year, and with a peasant voice in the government, his living conditions would improve.

He got the paper each Sunday after mass. While the small crowd of worshippers left the church, a young man in the group would pull the weekly edition of *The Sower* out from his trousers' waistband, which was covered by a loose-fitting blouse, and place it in Ioan's hand while discreetly looking in front of him. Without looking at him, Ioan would put the paper under his blouse while he continued his walk to the rear of the church in the midst of the exiting worshippers.

After reading the entire periodical, Ioan looked forlorn and then placed his hands over his face. "What's wrong?" asked his father.

"The leases with the peasants in a village in northern Moldavia were not renewed, and the peasants are revolting," said Ioan, after removing his hands from his face.

The following Sunday, Ioan waited impatiently through the long Orthodox service because his concern about the revolt distracted his attention from the chanting prayers of the priest. After receiving his copy of *The Sower* in the usual manner, he waited anxiously for Johanna to finish her weekly chat with her women friends.

When he finally got home, he eagerly took the illegal paper from his waistband while Johanna went out to fetch a chicken for their Sunday meal. The riot had spread south to Wallachia, and the ruling class was insisting that the Romanian government use its army to quell the rioters with lethal force. In this turmoil, Ioan's patron, Nicolae Iorga, and other intellectuals pleaded to the government for restraint.

The new information deepened Ioan's concern. Although Wallachia was a Romanian province, it was adjacent to Beba Veche's province of Banat. What would happen to his family if the riot continued in that direction? Because he was unable to control his destiny, he was completely frustrated. He became despondent and depressed.

The following edition of *The Sower* was even worse. The riot had been ended by the Romanian army. Estimates on the number of peasants that had been killed averaged ten thousand people. Ioan was confused by Iorga's editorials. On one hand, Iorga condemned the causes leading up to the riot, and on the other hand, he forgave the Romanian soldiers who shot the peasants to preserve order. Ioan's depression became worse. Iorga, his only hope for a better life, had now become a bitter disappointment.

In the summer of 1907, Ioan received a reply from his contact in St. Louis. The letter was about six pages long and verified all the facts that the agent had given to him. The contact encouraged him to come to America, work a year, and then bring his family there. After reading the letter carefully several times, Ioan began to think more favorably about moving to America. The conditions in Romania and Austria-Hungary left no hope for him, but moving to America, even with all its uncertainties, did have possibilities.

Up until this time, Ioan had not let anyone know his concerns about his family's future. At the evening meal, he told his family members that he was planning to move the family to America. They were stunned.

His father asked the obvious questions. "How do you expect to get there? Where will you get the money for you and the rest of your family? How will you be able to live there when you can't even speak English?"

Johanna and Elena kept silent. Decisions like this were customarily left to the men of a peasant family, and their concerns were already being addressed by Ioan's father. Traian, who was eight years old, was surprised and wide-eyed with interest.

For the rest of the evening and early into the night, Ioan explained about his visit to the agent at the fair in Sânnicolau Mare. He read the letter from his Romanian contact in America. He shared his calculations on how much he would earn in the first year, which would be enough for the rest of his immediate family to purchase passage tickets. With fewer mouths to feed, Stephan and Elena would have extra vegetables and meat to sell.

Ioan wasn't using his reasons to coerce an agreement from his wife and parents. His mind was made up. This was best for his family. It was his hope that if he shared all the information leading up to his decision, they would have less uncertainty about the outcome.

That night while lying in bed next to Johanna, he gazed up at the ceiling with an exhilarated feeling of freedom for the first time in his life. His bondage to the land was beginning to break.

The following day, Ioan drove his cart alone to Sânnicolau Mare and met with the agent to acquire all the information necessary so that he could obtain a passport and passage to America. Fortunately, there was a ship leaving from Trieste, Serbia, going to New York within the next thirty days.

The agent told Ioan to pack his bags and meet him in Sânnicolau Mare three days before his departure. From there, Ioan would be put on a train to Trieste, where he would board a ship named *Chemnitz*, which would arrive in New York on April 20, 1907, after a three-week voyage. In New York harbor, Ioan would be conveyed from the ship by barge to Ellis Island, where he would be processed through immigration. From Ellis Island, Ioan would be taken by immigration officials to a train station in New York and placed on a train bound for St. Louis.

"Before I do anything regarding your passport and ticket, you will need a physical examination," the agent said to him.

"Why?" said Ioan. "I feel fine. My health is good."

"I know that, but we need a doctor's certificate before I can book your passage. You will have another physical exam before you board the ship and another when you reach Ellis Island."

"I don't understand," Ioan replied with a puzzled look on his face.

"The problem is that if you don't pass the physical exam at Ellis Island, they will put you back on the ship and send you to Europe. The shipowners won't like that since the United States will not be paying for your passage."

"Where in Europe would they drop me off?"

"Probably Trieste, if that's the return voyage for the *Chemnitz*. If not, wherever the ship is scheduled to stop," said the agent with a tone of indifference.

"But how will I get back to Beba Veche?"

"That will be your problem. Now do you want to get the physical or not?" The agent was beginning to show some impatience.

Ioan was overwhelmed by the scenarios that lay ahead. He was beginning to have second thoughts about the whole idea. In a flash, he imagined himself in an unknown European port, unable to speak the language, and having no money for train fare to Beba Veche.

"Well?" said the agent, this time more vehemently.

"Let's go ahead," said Ioan weakly and after finally regaining some confidence. It was too late to turn back now.

Within the hour, the agent brought in the doctor that he had contracted for such occasions. The examination involved the doctor looking for skin problems, examining Ioan's throat and ears, and listening to his heart with a stethoscope.

"He's okay," the doctor told the agent without looking up while he filled out and signed the medical form.

"Your passport and steamship and train tickets will be ready in two weeks," said the agent. "Bring enough pocket money for your meals on the train. The train from Sânnicolau Mare to Trieste will take about twelve hours. The ship leaves Trieste on the afternoon of March 28. That means you must be here by noon on March 26 to get your passport and travel tickets in time to catch the train for Trieste, which will leave at 2:00 p.m., God willing."

"How long will the train ride be from New York to St. Louis?" asked Ioan.

"About one and a half days," replied the agent.

"How much are meals on the train?"

"A sandwich and a cup of coffee will cost you about one-fourth of a kronen," said the agent, who had answered that same question at least a hundred times before.

During the three-hour trip back to Beba Veche from Sânnicolau Mare, Ioan mentally processed all that needed to be done in the next two weeks. How would he send money from St. Louis to Johanna for her passage? How would he be able to communicate with his family during his year away? Had he taught Traian enough to read and write simple letters? How much would he need for meals on the train? Suppose the ship left several days late. Where would he stay? How much more would it cost?

It was late afternoon when Ioan arrived home. He got off the cart, and his father led the horse and cart back to the rear of the house. During the evening meal, Ioan revealed to his family what had taken place with the agent: the examination, the ship's departure date, and the date he would be leaving by train from Sânnicolau Mare. Little was said by the others, who by now were passively accepting Ioan's decision to move his family to America.

After the table was cleared, Ioan began his calculations.

1. Steamship passage: 180 kronen
2. Passport: 3 kronen
3. Train tickets (Europe):   3 kronen
4. Train tickets (America):   5 kronen
5. Meals on train (12):   4 kronen
   Total: 195 kronen

He then took the chest from the niche. The chest had 246 kronen, which included 6 kronen that were Traian's earnings from two seasons of tending goats. His Romanian contact in St. Louis said that he could earn 400 to 500 kronen in one year at the automobile plant. At that time, a krone was worth about twenty cents. His calculations gave him a surge of confidence that he was doing the right thing.

As the sun rose on March 25, 1907, Ioan drove the horse-drawn cart toward Sânnicolau Mare with Johanna at his side. Traian and his grandfather Stephan were seated on straw bales, which Ioan had placed in the back of the cart the night before. A suitcase with three changes of clothes, a bar of homemade soap, a straight razor, a shaving mug, a shaving brush, and a comb was beside them. Under his blouse, Ioan wore a money belt with sixty kronen.

Chiriac and Flora were at home with Elena. Hugs and kisses had already been exchanged with each of them in the midst of deep emotion and tears before Ioan climbed into the cart. His last goodbye was to his three-year-old son. Picking him up, drawing him close to his breast, and with tears in his eyes, Ioan said, "Now, Chiriac, you be a good boy while I am gone. Mind your mother, and you will come with them to America soon."

It was mid-morning when they arrived at the Sânnicolau Mare train station, which was a little early. Ioan was always early. A half hour later, the agent arrived with four young Romanian men carrying suitcases. They were the other men whom the agent had persuaded to immigrate to America on the *Chemnitz*. Ioan and Johanna were surprised and delighted that Ioan would not have to make the long journey alone. After introductions were made, a train whistle was heard in the distance. The tearful goodbyes began as the train pulled up to the station.

Traian was amazed at the sight of the engine with its loud bell, hissing steam, and huge iron wheels. He had never been that close to a train before. With a smile, he waved back at the engineer, forgetting for a moment that his father was going to be gone for a long time. Just as he had in Beba Veche, Ioan saved his last goodbye for Traian.

"Now, Traian, for the next year, you will be the man of the house. Take care of your mother and do not cause her any problems. Read my letters to her and write back what she wants me to know. We will all be together again soon."

While saying this, Ioan was gripping Traian's right hand and had his left hand on Traian's shoulder. When, "All aboard," was heard, Ioan let go of Traian's hand, grabbed him by the waist, lifted him up, and as he had done with Chiriac, kissed him on the lips with tears in his eyes. Ioan then boarded the train and started his journey to America.

Romanian peasant house, 1909

Romanian peasant museum, Bucharest

Nicolae Iorga

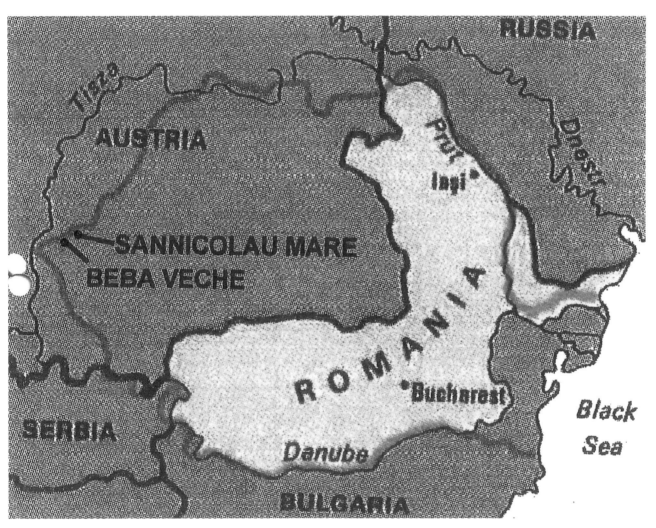

Romania, 1909

Romania today

CHAPTER 2
A FAMILY DIVIDED

The two-acre plot, which the family cultivated for its own use, was located about a mile away from Ioan's home in Beba Veche. One and a half acres were set aside for planting grain—wheat one year and corn during the next. About half of the yield was used for family consumption, and the remainder was sold. One half acre of the land was a vineyard. Grapes were a delicacy for the peasants, who used most of the harvest to make wine and liquor and the remainder for making jam. When they were ripe and ready for harvest, the grapes attracted thieves, who came in the middle of the night with large baskets to help themselves.

Stephan stood guard over the vineyard each night until the family harvested the grapes. When Traian turned six years old, he occasionally went with his grandfather to keep him company. They positioned themselves on high ground where they had a complete view of the vineyard as their eyes became adjusted to the darkness.

If a group of thieves showed up with their baskets, Stephan would take a large paper cap filled with gunpowder from his vest pocket and place it on top of the upside-down cast-iron skillet, which he had brought along. Then with a steel hammer, he struck the cap, producing a loud report that sounded like the warning blast of a shotgun. The thieves scattered. Traian liked to go on these guard assignments with this grandfather and really enjoyed it when Stephan handed Traian the hammer and told him to hit the cap.

Before Ioan left Romania, he made a visit to Father Dimitrie, who was the local Orthodox priest, and brought him a special gift for the church in the amount of fifty kronen. Ioan had taken the gift from the chest. Ioan had no bank account and kept all his savings in the wall niche. Father Dimitrie was surprised and extremely grateful for the gift because generous gifts were seldom given by peasants. He gave Ioan a special blessing.

After the blessing, Ioan told the priest of his plans to move his family to America. He then asked the father if he would tutor Traian in reading and writing Romanian, three hours a week, during the year while Ioan was in America. While tutoring Traian, Ioan also asked if Father Dimitrie would assist Traian in reading and responding to his correspondence from America.

Uncomfortable with his pastor's initial hesitation, Ioan quickly sweetened the pot with a promise of another fifty kronen to be given to the church after he received his first paycheck in America. Father Dimitrie said that he would be able to help Traian with his literacy in the Romanian language.

While walking back home from the pastor's residence, Ioan began focusing on his next challenge: sending money to his family members and arranging for their passports and travel to America. He decided that he would deal with that problem after he got to America, with the help of the Romanian contact. *Other people have done it, so why can't I?* he thought as his self-confidence began to build.

On April 23, 1907, at 10:00 a.m., Ioan arrived at Union Station in St. Louis. After departing the train, he sat down on one of the benches in the large waiting area. Overall, the trip had not been as bad as he had expected it to be.

On the train from Sânnicolau Mare to Trieste, he met with one of the four other Romanians. He was a young man named Vasille, who was a recent graduate from the University of Timisoara. Timisoara was a relatively large city with a population of over fifty-thousand people. It was located sixty miles north of Beba Veche. Vasille's father was a tailor in Timisoara. His father's brother had immigrated to New York in 1905. Vasille had a limited command of the English language. During the three-week voyage, Vasille taught Ioan a few English phrases like, "How much does that cost?" "Where is the men's restroom?" "Will you take me to this address?"

Since Vasille's uncle lived in New York, they separated there. Ioan was put on a train to St. Louis by the immigration officials at Ellis Island. He had undergone his final physical examination and the routine vetting there.

After a few minutes rest on the bench in the huge waiting room at Union Station, Ioan reached into his money belt and pulled out the name and address of his Romanian contact in St. Louis. He left the waiting room and went up the short flight of stairs to the street level, where a number of horse-drawn cabs were waiting for customers.

As he held the name and address of his contact in his right hand, he signaled a cabdriver, who came down from his open seat at the rear of his cab. After several minutes of strained communication, Ioan was reasonably sure that the cabdriver knew where he wanted to go and what the fare would be. The ten-cent fare was well within the ten dollars and fifty-three cents he had in his money belt.

The trip from Union Station to the address of the contact took about twenty minutes. "Here we are," said the cabdriver as he opened the door to the cab and helped Ioan with his luggage. Reaching into his money belt again, Ioan counted out the fare and a 10 percent tip, which Vasille had said was customary.

As the cabdriver drove off, Ioan surveyed his surroundings. It was a retail neighborhood with small businesses on the ground floor and living quarters above. The street was paved with brick, and there was a set of streetcar tracks in the middle of it. Ioan had noticed the streetcars with some amazement and curiosity during his ride in the cab. At the address of his final destination, there was a restaurant and tavern with the customary living quarters above.

Ioan stood outside contemplating what to do next. Would his contact be inside? If not, would there be anyone inside who could speak Romanian? With a shrug, Ioan opened the door to the tavern, walked up to the bar, and without saying a word, handed the bartender the piece of paper with his contact's name and address on it.

After glancing at the crumpled piece of paper, the bartender's face lit up with a big smile. While reaching out to shake Ioan's hand, he said to him in Romanian, "Welcome to St. Louis. I have been expecting you." The bartender, whose name was Bucur (Joy in Romanian), was Ioan's contact. Ioan's trip had finally ended.

On May 7, 1907, Ioan's first letter from St. Louis reached Beba Veche.

> *My dearest Johanna and family,*
>
> *It has been a long trip but not as difficult as I had expected. My contact in America owns a tavern and restaurant. He and his family live in rooms above the restaurant. I slept there on my first night in St. Louis.*
>
> *I am now staying in a large home with ten other single Romanian men. We share the rent, cooking, and cleaning. My Romanian contact, Bucur, has a son Traian's age. His name is also Bucur.*
>
> *I work at Ford Motor Company and paint cars. My pay is good. My living expenses are less than I expected. Within the next twelve months, I expect to have enough saved to bring the rest of my beautiful family over so that we can all be together again. You will love America.*
>
> *With all my love,*
>
> *Ioan*

Traian had no trouble reading the letter to the family. Afterward, he took out his writing tablet and pencil, which he would use in school, and awaited his mother's reply. Remembering that his father had told him at the train station in Sânnicolau Mare that he was now the head of the family and with a diplomatic combination of respect and authority, he told his mother that she should reply soon because it would take thirty-eight days for their letter to reach St. Louis.

"How would you know that?" asked Johanna.

"By counting the days from the postage date on the letter Papa sent," Traian said, beaming with pride.

Within a week, Traian brought the reply letter to Father Dimitrie when he went for his Romanian grammar lesson. Maintaining his ego as man of the house, Traian wrote the letter in first person with a salutation of "Dear Father" and a closing of "Your obedient, loving son." The body of the letter contained the family's thankfulness for Ioan's doing well, a report on everyone's health, and a bit of social news involving Aunt Lena, Johanna's younger sister who had just become engaged to Georgio, a young peasant in Beba Veche. Traian also offered reassurance to his father that his Romanian grammar lessons with Father Dimitrie were going well.

Although Johanna was illiterate, she was intelligent and had deep feelings for Ioan. She immediately understood Traian's method of figuring out how long it would take Ioan to receive their letter. She was proud of Traian for being able to do that. As far as her feelings were concerned, it was awkward for her to express them in the reply letter, which was dominated by Traian's ego and left no room for the deep feelings she had for Ioan. Her intimate feelings for Ioan could not be dictated to her son.

In early July of 1907, Beba Veche was struck by an epidemic of influenza that infected over a hundred of its people. Men and women of all ages contracted the disease. Within a month, eleven people had died. Among them had been Lena's fiancé, Georgio.

At his funeral, Father Dimitrie chanted Orthodox hymns while swinging a censer, which emitted perfumed white clouds over Georgio's wooden casket. Lena and Johanna were sitting in the front pew and were sobbing. Elena was sitting next to Johanna and was holding her hand. Because she was twenty years older, Elena had experienced many more deaths of those who had been close to her and was not crying. Her emotions were calloused. Traian was sitting next to Elena and was not crying. He was the man of the house. Men did not cry.

On August 7, 1907, Ioan's second letter reached Beba Veche. Traian read it to the family. The letter was somewhat longer than the first. It mostly covered his growing relationship with his contact, Bucur, who was a quasi leader in the small Romanian community in St. Louis. Ioan again mentioned meeting Bucur's son, who reminded him of Traian. He also said he had opened a bank savings account and put money into it regularly. The letter ended with his expressions of love and longing for his family.

> *Dearest Papa,*
>
> *Your second letter came to Beba Veche on the seventh day of August. I am sorry to give you bad news, but our town has been struck by a spreading sickness. Eleven people have died. Georgio was one of them. Lena and Momma are very sad. Lena is living with us now.*
>
> *Momma said she loves you and misses you. I miss you too. Flora and Chiriac miss you too. Your obedient and loving son,*
>
> *Traian*

This time, Johanna got her feelings about Ioan into Traian's letter. After Traian wrote that he missed his father, she also told him to include Flora and Chiriac.

The Romanian community in St. Louis was located in Soulard, between Third and Twelfth Streets, and not far from the Mississippi River. The first Romanian immigrant arrived in 1897. By 1908, there were about thirty Romanians living in the area, mostly single men along with a few married men who had families in Europe. Several Romanian families had established themselves.

Bucor was well-known in the community. He made a point of seeing that new Romanian immigrants found employment and housing when they first arrived. He also lent them small sums of money when needed, to hold them over until payday. He had empathy but was very businesslike in these transactions. He charged interest on loans not repaid within thirty days.

He encouraged all immigrants to learn to speak English as soon as possible and to become citizens. However, he still wanted to retain Romanian traditions and its heritage in St. Louis. To do this, he used his tavern/café, which he called The Place. Romanians met there on Sundays.

The meetings began with prayers and hymns in Romanian led by a layman, who had been assigned for that Sunday. The worship service was followed by a social hour. This included a one-dish meal of Romanian cooking and drinks from the bar. A dish for voluntary donations was placed at the serving table, which included tea and coffee; however, they were charged when they ordered drinks from the bar.

Occasionally, the religious service was performed by a traveling Romanian Orthodox priest. One might say that this was the beginning of Saint Thomas the Apostle Romanian Orthodox Church. In 1935, Bucur's son served as chairman of the committee that founded the Romanian church, which started as a house church at 1477 Missouri Avenue. The church later moved to a converted funeral home at 5624 South Compton Avenue and then to its present location, the beautiful church at 6501 Nottingham Avenue.

Ioan quickly became accustomed to America. The language was not as difficult to learn as he had expected it to be. Since the Romanian language had come from Latin roots, he found that many English nouns and verbs were similar to Romanian ones. Out of necessity, he learned the English commands that his foreman at the Ford plant would give him: "Ioan, come here," "Ioan, it's lunchtime," "Ioan, lunchtime is over," and "Ioan, watch me. Here is how you do it."

Fortunately, one of his immigrant roommates who worked with him had come to America six months earlier than Ioan had. He helped Ioan clarify any directions from the foreman that he didn't understand.

In addition, during Sunday social hour, Bucur encouraged the new immigrants to converse in English. "The sooner you learn the language, the quicker you will be able to earn more money."

Ioan's bank account continued to grow faster than he had expected. With Bucur's help, he learned how to send money to Johanna. He also sent a letter to Father Dimitrie, thanking him for teaching Traian. In his letter, Ioan asked Father Dimitrie to assist Johanna in depositing the certified bank checks, which he had mailed to her, in a special account in Sânnicolau Mare Bank. He also asked the father to help her withdraw the money and to assist her in securing passports and making travel arrangements to America when the time came. Ioan enclosed a five-dollar bill as a donation to the church.

August 6, 1908

My dearest Johanna and family,

With God's help, our family will be together again in about eight months. I miss you all so much. I have made arrangements at a bank in St. Louis to start sending money to you and have written a letter to Father Dimitrie asking him to help with your passports and travel arrangements. I have arranged for checks to be put into the Sânnicolau Mare bank under Johanna's name. Traian, teach your mother how to write her name so that she can draw the money out when it is needed for travel costs. You will love America.

I miss my family so much,

Ioan

Early in September of 1908, Chiriac started vomiting and told Johanna that his head hurt. She gave him some fig syrup to settle his stomach and put her hand on his forehead. "He's got a fever," she said to Lena. "I'm going to give him a bath. Put some warm water in the tub."

Lena poured several quarts of hot water from the kettle into the large copper vat that was used for bathing and making apple sauce. Then she added several quarts of cold water to make the temperature of the water lukewarm. "Come on, Chiriac. Let's get you into the bath," she said. But Chiriac could not move his legs. Lena went to his bed to lift him out. He screamed in pain when she grabbed his legs.

Chiriac recovered quickly from his headache and nausea but could not move his legs for a week. During this time, Johanna massaged his legs gently and bathed them with warm, moist cloths several times a day to give him comfort. Two weeks later, the pain was gone, and with some effort, he was able to move his legs. Although he was still not able to walk, Johanna did notice a slight improvement in his condition each week. In a month, he would be able to walk with crutches.

On February 5, 1909, Ioan's eighth letter was opened by Traian after the family's evening meal.

My Dear Family,

There is now enough money in the Sânnicolau bank for you all to come to America. Also bring Lena. There are at least ten Romanian bachelors here in St. Louis. One should make a good husband for her. Lena will be able to help Johanna with the three children during the trip.

I have found a nice home to rent for our family. It has two bedrooms, a kitchen, and a living room. It also has running water. Johanna will not need to go to the well for water.

There is a ship leaving Fiume on March 6. Its name is Carpathia. See Father Dimitrie. Have him go to the bank with you. Draw out the money. With this last check along with the others I have sent, there should be 862 kronen. This will be needed by Father Dimitrie for your train tickets and passage on the Carpathia. This should also cover the cost for your passports. I have already given Father Dimitrie money for his help. He should not be expecting anything more from you.

The cost for your transportation and passports will be 580 kronen. The remaining 282 kronen will be needed for meals on the train. Do not spend more than one and a half kronens for each meal in Europe and thirty cents for each meal in America. You should have thirty dollars when you leave Ellis Island and board the train for St. Louis. You will all need to get medical examinations before your ship tickets can be bought. There will be another examination before you board the ship and another one when you arrive in America. My heart will be filled with joy when we can all be together again.

My love to all,

Ioan

On February 10, 1909, Stephan stopped the horse-drawn wagon in front of Father Dimitrie's house. Seated next to him in the front of the wagon was Johanna and Lena. Traian, Flora, and Chiriac were in the straw-filled back.

Over the past few months, Chiriac had shown continued but slow improvement. However, he still walked with a noticeable limp. When Father Dimitrie came out, Lena gave up her seat to him and joined the children in the back of the wagon.

By noon, they had arrived at the agent's office in Sânnicolau for their physical examinations, which were required for the purchase of steamship tickets. Traian went first, followed by Flora and Lena. As the doctor was filling out their forms, Johanna walked in carrying Chiriac.

"Why are you carrying him?" asked the doctor.

"He had a little problem last September, but he is almost well now," Johanna replied.

"Can he walk?"

"Oh yes," Johanna said while setting Chiriac down. "Show the doctor how well you can walk now."

"You mean there was a time after he got sick that he couldn't walk?" Little by little and with penetrating questions from the doctor, Johanna revealed Chiriac's symptoms since the first day of his illness as the doctor made notes on the examination sheet.

"You see how good he is doing. In a year, he will be walking normally," Johanna said, trying to convince the doctor.

After the doctor finished Johanna's examination, he completed his paperwork and gave it to the agent for booking passage. The agent quickly read through the examination papers and without looking up, said with complete indifference, "Everything looks fine, but the cripple can't go!"

On the doctor's desk was a pamphlet from the Cunard Line warning that the following people would not be admitted to the United States:

Persons with infectious diseases such as trachoma, focus, lupus, etc., persons with a police record, persons who believe and support polygamy, single women with children or single pregnant women, and all persons who may have to rely on public charity for survival such as the blind, paralyzed, deaf and dumb, crippled, etc.

Johanna was stunned. At the beginning of Chiriac's illness when he had no feeling in his legs, she had been worried about his passing the physical examination. But with his continued improvement, her concerns had abated. "Why?" screamed Johanna.

"It should be obvious to you. The child can't walk."

"He can walk. Show him Chiriac. See? He has no need for crutches!"

"Lady, the doctor's report says that he's crippled. I can't do anything about his report. You should be thankful we caught it here. What would you do if they caught it in Fiume before you boarded ship? Worse yet, what if it wasn't caught until he got to America? If that happened, he would be put back on the ship and returned to Europe. Who would go with him?"

Father Dimitrie placed his hand on Johanna's shoulder as she sobbed. "He is right, Johanna. It is a blessing that they stopped him here. In a year, Chiriac will be walking without a limp, and I promise you that I will help you find a way to get him to America."

Stephan then came up and put his arms around Johanna, who received little comfort from Father Dimitrie's words. "Elena and I will take good care of Chiriac. There is nothing more that we can do. We must leave for Beba now so that we will be back before dark."

On the way home, Father Dimitrie sat in the back of the wagon with the children while Elena sat in front with Johanna. Elena held Johanna's hand and comforted her. Johanna dried her eyes, drew strength from Elena, and resolved to accept what had to be.

CHAPTER 3
THE JOURNEY TO AMERICA

This was the day: March 2, 1909. At 5:00 a.m., their four suitcases were packed: one for Traian, one for Flora, one for Lena, and one for Johanna. Stephan was stroking the neck of the old horse while Elena was crying, hugging, and kissing the four travelers. Elena then handed Johanna a picture of herself and Chiriac. The picture had been taken a month before Chiriac had been stricken with his crippling disease. "Here is something so that you will remember Chiriac. Keep it close to your heart while you pray for his complete recovery so that someday soon, you will see him again."

"We must go now," Stephan said softly with a lump in his throat as he climbed up into the cart.

Johanna, who was on the verge of tears, picked up Chiriac and kissed him. "Now, you be a good boy and mind Baba Elena," she said while putting him down. As she climbed into the cart next to Stephan and Lena, the tears broke through. She worried that she would ever see Chiriac again.

The trip to Sânnicolau was uneventful for Traian. He had made it many times in the past. Now he was anxious to ride the train.

When they arrived at the station, Stephan stopped the horse. It was 8:00 a.m., and they were a half hour ahead of the train's arrival. The agent with their passports, train tickets to Fiume, steamship tickets, and train tickets from New York to St. Louis was waiting for them at the station. As he handed the packet of tickets to Johanna, he said, "Now keep this with you at all times and never leave it out of your sight. The four train tickets to Fiume are on the top. Give them to the conductor when you board the train."

Johanna took the packet from his hand without speaking or even looking at him. In a flash, she immediately recalled her unpleasant experience with him the last time they had met. His calling Chiriac a "cripple" and his lack of concern for her feelings had been burned deeply into her memory. She hated him and was glad to see him leave.

After the agent had gone, they were on their own.

"If the train is on time, it should be here in fifteen minutes. Let's see what's in the packet," Stephan said.

"I can help you, Momma," Traian said as Johanna started to hand the packet to Stephan. As man of the house, Traian took the packet from his mother's hands and carefully opened it.

"Here are the train tickets to Fiume, Momma. Put them in your purse and give them to the conductor when we board the train. These other large things in the thicker envelopes are our passports and ship tickets. We will have to show them to someone before we get on the ship. The other envelope has tickets from New York to St. Louis. Keep them in the packet with the passports."

Then they heard the train whistle. The train was on time. As it pulled into the station with the bell ringing and hissing steam coming from relief valves, Traian waved at the engineer, who returned Traian's wave. He looked like the same engineer who had taken Traian's father away a year ago.

After hugs were given and sad goodbyes were said to Stephan, they prepared to board the train. Traian, again showing his authority as man of the house, suggested that Lena carry his mother's suitcase, which would allow her to handle the tickets more conveniently. Traian said he would carry Flora's suitcase. Johanna and Lena smiled at each other.

Because Johanna was in a pampering mood, she said, "That's a good idea, Traian. Thank you for thinking of your mother."

The train trip to Fiume was exciting for Traian. It was a stark contrast to the transportation he had been accustomed to in Beba Veche, which had been a horse-drawn cart. Johanna found two empty seats facing each other and with the help of Traian and Lena, placed their suitcases on the luggage rack above them. Traian quickly claimed his seat next to the window. Flora, being several years younger, felt a little insecure and took an aisle seat next to Lena, who was sitting across from Traian.

After two quick toots of the steam whistle, the train began chugging forward. Soon it reached a speed of over fifty miles an hour. Traian, with his forehead against the window, watched with amazement as the landscape whizzed by.

The conductor came down the aisle and said, "Tickets please," in Romanian, Hungarian, and Serbian. Johanna reached into her purse and handed them to the conductor, who punched them, tore the receipts from their perforations, and handed them back to Johanna.

Bewildered, Johanna turned to Traian and asked, "What am I supposed to do with these?"

"Keep them in your purse. They show that you have paid for your tickets if you ever need to get off the train and get back on again before we get to Fiume," Traian said with authoritative confidence.

"How did you know that?" Johanna responded with a surprised look on her face.

"Since I am the man of the house, I am expected to know these things," Traian replied as he turned his head back toward the window. Actually, Traian had been coached on what to expect by Father Dimitrie in his last tutoring session. He chose not to reveal this to his mother, hoping to impress her with his intelligence.

At around noon, a vendor with a tray of sandwiches and cakes came through the car and said in a loud voice again in three languages, "Sandwiches and cakes. Sandwiches and cakes."

Johanna stopped him as he came up to her. "How much?" she asked.

"What kind of money do you have?"

"Kronen," Johanna responded.

"One-fourth a kronen for a sandwich and one-fourth a kronen for a cake."

"Too much," Johanna replied. "I will give you one and a half kronens for four sandwiches and four cakes."

Ignoring her, the vendor went on while calling in a loud voice, "Sandwiches and cakes. Sandwiches and cakes."

Johanna was bewildered and embarrassed. She had been accustomed to bartering when making a purchase. The seller would always offer a price, and the buyer would make an offer. Then a friendly negotiation would begin, and eventually, the two would arrive at an agreed upon price. It always happened that way at the fruit and vegetable market on Saturdays in Beba Veche.

About a half hour later, the vendor was making his way back, but his tray was nearly empty. When he entered the car, this time Johanna opened her purse, took out two kronen, and waited for him to pass. As he came by, she said, "I will have four sandwiches and four cakes," and she handed him the money.

The vendor handed her four sandwiches and three cakes. While giving her back one-fourth of a krone, the vendor said, "I only have three cakes left."

Johanna handed a sandwich and a cake to Lena, Flora, and Traian and kept a sandwich for herself. Traian, who had been observing his mother's embarrassment in her bartering attempt, felt sorry for her and handed her his cake saying, "Here, Momma. Take my cake. I am not very hungry."

At 4:00 p.m., the train arrived at the station in Fiume. As they left the train, Traian asked the conductor how to get to the pier where the *Carpathia* was docked. The conductor told him, "You will need to take a cab," and pointed to the line of horse-drawn cabs that were parked at the front of the station and were waiting for customers.

As Traian went up to the first cab, he asked the driver if he spoke Romanian. "A little," the driver replied.

"The four of us have tickets on the ship *Carpathia*. It leaves at 8:00 p.m. How much is the fare?"

"One krone," said the driver.

"How long will it take?" asked Traian.

"About thirty minutes," replied the driver.

"Good. Take us there," Traian said as he ushered his family into the seats of the cab.

The event at the Fiume train station was just as Father Dimitrie had predicted. Traian's uncertainty began to decrease. His confidence as man of the house increased. He was becoming, if anything, overconfident.

When they arrived at the pier, Traian asked his mother to give the driver one krone for the fare and one-tenth of a krone for the 10 percent tip as Father Dimitrie had instructed. Traian's request to his mother was firm. He did not want his mother to even consider bartering.

There were several large lines of people waiting to board the ship. At the ends of the lines, there were signs designating nationalities. Traian led the family to the end of the Hungarian line. Although their family was of Romanian descent, they were citizens of Austria-Hungary. Here again, Traian followed Father Dimitrie's instructions.

In about a half hour, they finally got to the front of the line. This was not the boarding area of the ship. It was a building at the shore end of the pier where all passengers to America received their second physical examination prior to boarding the ship. There were two dozen people sitting in the waiting room on twelve-foot-long benches. Two benches were against the wall, and two benches were back-to-back in the middle of the room. As passengers went into the examination room, people scooted up the bench, allowing passengers outside to come in and seat themselves.

An hour and a half later, Traian's family was at the head of the examination line. It was 6:00 p.m. They still had two hours before the ship's departure time. The examination only took five minutes per person. This time, there were no problems. By 6:30 p.m., they were met by an agent who checked their passports, health certificates, and steamship tickets.

Although the vetting process had taken several hours, it had been easy to understand since most of the people giving directions spoke several languages, one of which was Romanian. This was a requirement of all employees on the steamship line.

They followed the line, left the examination building, and went to the pier where the *Carpathia* was docked. As they went out the door from the building to the pier, Traian's eyes opened in amazement at the size of the ship that was docked on the left side of the pier. The imposing black hull, which was well over five hundred feet long, stretched from the shore to the seaward end of the pier.

They approached the stern of the ship where Traian caught a view of the huge black hull, which was pierced with portholes that admitted light to the lower decks. The middle two-thirds of the ship was a white superstructure with larger windows. At the top of this superstructure, there was a row of big lifeboats. This was a sobering reminder that ships had been known to sink.

Dominating the center of this gigantic mass of steel was a huge red smokestack that was over sixteen feet in diameter and rose at least fifty feet above the top of the uppermost deck. The upper ten feet of the smokestack was painted black. Traian gazed at the huge ship with amazement.

There were two covered gangways leading from the pier to the first open deck of the ship. The first gangway was located about 150 feet forward of the stern for the convenience of the first-class passengers. The second gangway was another two hundred feet forward toward the bow of the ship, where the second- and third-class passengers were being directed in several languages by the ship's employees.

As they entered the gangway, Johanna showed their steamship tickets to the ship's officer, as directed by Traian. Johanna was beginning to get tired of Traian's authoritative nature and was contemplating how she was going to put him in his proper place and regain control of her family.

Sensing his mother's impatience with his authoritative manner when she had looked at him sternly during his last directive, Traian began his role as big brother. He grabbed Flora's bag as she was struggling with it halfway up the gangway. Flora, who was only seven years old at the time, had inherited her mother's physical strength, but the heavy bag was a little too much for her. In fact, the two bags proved to be too much for Traian as well. By the time they got to the top of the gangway, Lena was carrying Flora's bag.

At the top of the gangway, they were met by a steward, who checked the deck and cabin number on their tickets. In Romanian, he directed them to the stairwell that led down to their assigned deck. At the top of the stairs, they were met by another steward. After looking at their tickets, he said in Romanian, "Right now, you are on the upper deck. The next deck below us is the main deck. Below that is the lower deck. That is where your cabin is."

When they reached the lower deck, they were met by another steward, who directed them to a narrow corridor that ran perpendicular to the length of the ship and had a porthole at the end. The limited amount of natural light was supplemented by electric lights, which were powered by the ship's generators.

Their compartment was the last one on the left, at the end of the corridor. It was about eight feet long by eight feet wide. It had double bunks on each side and a washbasin on the back wall with a water tank above it. Above the washbasin, there was an electric light, which could be operated by a switch inside the door.

"Put the suitcases under the beds, and let's go to the dining room on the deck above and eat. The steward said they will stop serving at eight o'clock," Johanna said sternly as she gave Traian a penetrating stare. Johanna decided it was time for her to take charge.

The dining room was located one deck below where they had boarded the ship. The gangway was now taken away as men on the shore were removing ropes from the pier posts in preparation for departure. Johanna firmly grabbed Traian by the arm. Distracted by the activity on the pier, he had begun to stray away from the family. Johanna had now assumed control.

The dining room was large. It seated over three hundred people at long tables with deck-mounted swivel chairs on each side. The walls were wood-paneled, and the floor was covered with linoleum. They made it for the last seating. Johanna was pleasantly surprised at the quality of the meal: fried lamb, potatoes, pastry cheese bread, wine, and figs.

As was the custom in Beba Veche, children were allowed a few ounces of wine at meals. Johanna's mind went back some seven years to the time when she had dunked Traian in the horse trough as she poured a little wine into Traian's cup.

After they had finished their evening meal, Johanna said, "We will now go and see the rest of the ship."

As they reached the door to leave the dining room, Traian asked the steward, who was standing by the door, "Where are we permitted to go?"

The steward replied in Romanian, "You are allowed to go one deck above."

"What is up there?" asked Traian.

"There is a nice ladies' lounge with settees, chairs, and tables and a men's smoking room. There is also an open deck with chairs."

As they left the dining room, they entered a wide corridor that had ladies' restrooms on its starboard side and men's restrooms on its port side. "We will now use the restroom before going up to the next deck, Traian. You will have to use the men's restroom, which is over there," Johanna said as she pointed toward the other side of the ship.

As Traian entered the men's restroom, he noticed that there was a line of toilet compartments on the far wall. Two of them were larger rooms and each had a bathtub. On the wall to his right were washbasins with mirrors above them. After using the one empty toilet compartment available, Traian went into an empty tub room and began playing with the water faucets and light switch in utter fascination. Hot water came from one faucet, and cold water came from the next faucet. No one had to go to the well for water. No one had to heat water on the stove. He pushed the light switch up, and the light turned on. He pushed the light switch down, and the light turned off. His playing was suddenly interrupted by an older man who wanted to take a bath, so he went to a bench outside the ladies' restroom to wait for the women.

When they came out, Johanna told the group that they would now go up to the next deck and look around. With some embarrassment, Traian followed his mother's orders to go with them into the ladies' lounge. He felt more comfortable when he saw several other boys his age in the room. The room was a pleasant surprise. As the steward described, it had a large number of tables and chairs with women seated at them, chatting with each other. Some were knitting. There were also a number of upholstered lounge chairs with ladies stretched out in comfortable resting positions.

The *Carpathia*, which had been launched four years earlier, advertised comfortable accommodations for third-class passengers and was a strong competitor for the immigrant-passenger market. Johanna was pleased to find out that during the long voyage, there would be a more pleasant place for the family than the tiny cabin and crowded dining room.

With Johanna's permission, Traian left the ladies' lounge to see the men's smoking room on the other side of the ship. He did not stay long. The room was furnished in the same manner as the ladies' room, but the thick haze of smoke burned his eyes. He returned to the ladies' room just as Johanna, Lena, and Flora were about to leave and explore the open promenade at the front of the ship, where the third-class passengers were allowed to go for fresh air.

The promenade deck was open to the weather and extended about one hundred feet from the bulkhead to the bow of the ship. In the middle of it was a mast, which was one hundred feet tall. It had guylines to the deck's edge on each side of the ship. In front of the mast was a cargo hatch about twenty-four feet long by twelve feet wide, which protruded three feet above the open deck. By this time, the ship had left the pier, and it was well underway. It was heading west in the Adriatic Sea. The sun had set several hours before and the light from the moon and stars reflected on the foaming waves as it cut its way through the dark blue sea.

Johanna and Lena were stunned at what they were experiencing. They stood speechless as they absorbed the beauty they were looking at. Traian and Flora stood next to them and held hands. The only sound was the ship making its way through the Adriatic Sea.

All four slept well the first night at sea in their tiny cabin. Traian chose the upper bunk above Flora while Lena slept in the one above Johanna's bunk. Traian got up first. He washed his face and hands at the washbasin located at the end of the cabin, which only had cold water. Following that, he took off his nightshirt and put on the clothes he had worn the previous day. After he had dressed himself, he told Johanna that he wanted to go out in the corridor and look out of the porthole. This allowed the women in the cabin to have privacy while they got dressed; a procedure that continued throughout the voyage.

After breakfast, the movement of the ship began taking its toll on a number of passengers at breakfast. Stewards began passing out paper bags to those who were becoming seasick and were about to lose their breakfast.

Although Traian and Flora were spared, Johanna and Lena were beginning to feel nauseated and asked for the bags. Johanna began to perspire. She took off her shawl, carefully folded it up, and set it on the floor beside her chair. She then signaled the steward to give her a bag, which came none too soon. After losing her breakfast, she handed the bag to Traian, who deposited it in the nearest trash container.

When he returned, Johanna told Traian to take Flora up to the promenade deck to get some fresh air while she and Lena went to the cabin to lie down. She then reached down to pick up her shawl. It was gone. Too sick to bother about it, Johanna went below with Lena, where they both remained sick for the next two days. During this time, Traian looked after Flora by taking her to the meals and then up to the promenade deck where Traian continued to be mesmerized by the waves.

After several days, Johanna and Lena were feeling better and were able to go up to the promenade deck for fresh air. Johanna was now able to focus on finding her shawl. Like her special shoes that she had kept under her bed in Beba Veche, the shawl was also dear to her. She had knitted it when she had been sixteen years old. It had drawn many compliments when she had worn it to church and on other occasions.

It truly was a work of art. The field of black wool was textured with flowers from special tightly knotted yarn, and the edges were fringed with small loops of braided yarn. Johanna was convinced that there was no other shawl like it among the 1,100 third-class women passengers. She promised herself that she would find it.

Without revealing her intentions to the others, she began her search by making regular, casual walks around the dining room during meals, up to the ladies' room, and then on the promenade deck. After two days, she recognized her shawl on the back of a middle-aged passenger on the promenade deck.

Overcome with the thrill of seeing her precious shawl again and fired up with determination to repossess it, Johanna approached the woman from behind and snatched the shawl from her back without saying a word. The surprised woman suddenly turned around. Seeing the fire in Johanna's eyes, she decided to avoid any confrontation and walked away as if nothing had happened. Traian, who had witnessed the event, was a little embarrassed. However, he had a feeling of security, which often came when his mother exhibited her strength.

On March 27, 1909, after twenty-one days at sea, the Carpathia steamed up the wide entrance of the Hudson River. It was about 6:00 p.m. The four of them stood on the promenade deck and looked north toward the skyline of Manhattan, with its fifteen-story-tall buildings. Between the ship and Manhattan Island, Traian saw a small island with a tall green statue of a woman extending a torch in her right hand toward the sky.

At the mouth of the Hudson River, the Carpathia stopped and dropped its anchor. As had been the procedure for the previous ten years, a team of doctors and immigration officials boarded the ship. This team met with the captain and officers of the ship, who gave them lists of the passengers who would be taken to Ellis Island for further vetting.

The immigration officials were also given the names of sick passengers being attended to by the ship's doctors. These passengers were immediately removed from the ship and were ferried to the hospital at Ellis Island. The ship's officers also identified for the immigration officials, passengers of a suspicious nature, who were also taken to Ellis Island for detainment while their identities were being verified.

After they finished their evening meal, Traian asked his mother's permission to go back on the promenade deck. This she allowed after telling him not to stay too long. By this time, the sun had set, and the skyline of Manhattan had become ablaze with electric lights. The green statue of the lady holding the torch was illuminated with search lights from the ground, and the torch in her right hand glowed with a bright orange light. Traian was amazed by all the lights. The sight of it exceeded his wildest imagination of what America would be like. He could not wait to get off the ship.

Carpathia at Sea

Carpathia State room

Carpathia Third class dining room.

CHAPTER 4
ELLIS ISLAND

The following morning, Traian got up early, washed his face, dressed, and went up to the promenade deck. He saw a small boat approaching the *Carpathia*, which was anchored just outside New York Harbor. After the small boat came alongside the big ship, the connecting lines were attached. Then Traian watched several men and one woman board the ship. They were people from the State of New York Quarantine Division. Their job was to remove passengers who were sick and required isolation from the ship. Cholera, smallpox, typhoid fever, and even leprosy were the diseases that the quarantine officers looked for.

Sick and infected passengers were removed from the ship and were taken to Hoffman Island, which was in the lower bay outside the Verrazzano Narrows, for further examination. If people were found to be dangerously infected, they were sent to the chief quarantine hospital on the neighboring Swinburne Island. During the quarantine inspection, a yellow flag was raised on the ship and then lowered when all infected passengers had been removed.

After watching the small group board, Traian went back to the small stateroom where his mother, sister, and aunt were up and dressed. After they had breakfast together, Traian went back to the promenade deck while the rest of the family went to the ladies' sitting room on the deck below.

On the promenade deck, Traian found a vantage point where he could see that the small vessel was still attached to the *Carpathia*'s hull. A short time later, he noticed the same group of people leaving the *Carpathia* and boarding the small boat with *Carpathia* passengers. This was followed by five passengers boarding it, assisted by a few of *Carpathia*'s crew members. Lastly, two passengers were carried aboard on stretchers. After all the sick passengers were aboard the small boat and the crew members had returned to the *Carpathia*, the mooring lines were withdrawn.

As the small boat steamed away, it signaled to the *Carpathia* with its small steam whistle. The *Carpathia* responded with a much louder blast, which startled Traian. Looking in the direction of the sound, Traian noticed a yellow flag, which he had not seen before, being lowered from the mast of the *Carpathia*.

At the noon meal, Traian told Johanna about the small vessel and the removal of the sick passengers. After listening with intense interest, Johanna said, "This is a good sign. America is looking after sick passengers first and getting them to the hospital as soon as possible." She had strong nurturing instincts and quarantining infectious diseases never entered her mind.

By 1:00 p.m., Traian was back on the promenade deck and this time saw a small cutter approaching. After reaching the *Carpathia* and being lashed to it in a manner similar to the previous vessel, Traian noticed a small group of people leave the small cutter and board the *Carpathia*. The people boarding this time were US government officials from the Immigration Division of Boarding. They usually consisted of two immigrant inspectors, two doctors, four clerks, four interpreters, and one matron.

They first met with the ship's officers, obtained a handwritten copy of the ship's passenger list, and sought passenger information from observations of the ship's officers during the voyage. They were looking for suspicious passengers: people who had caused problems during the voyage or appeared to be sick and single women in steerage class. After that, the boarding officials would meet with the ship's officers to single out possible passengers who might be questionable immigrants.

At 2:00 p.m., Traian heard an announcement over the ship's loudspeaker: "All passengers must undergo an inspection by officials of the United States government before they can leave the ship. The inspecting officers and translators will be in the ladies' sitting room for second- and third-class passengers starting at 3:00 p.m." The announcement was made in four different languages: Hungarian, Serbian, Romanian, and Bulgarian.

After hearing the announcement, Traian left the promenade deck and went immediately to the ladies' sitting room on the deck below. The room was being cleared for the officials from the immigration division. Two inspection locations were being set up while two lines were being organized by two crew members. One line was for men, and the other line was for women and children. Directions were being given by the two crew members in four different languages.

Traian found his family in the women's line and was told by Johanna to stand behind Flora. Johanna had been told by another third-class passenger about the inspection and was advised not to give any more information than what was being asked.

"Now listen to me, Traian," she said while grasping his arm. "I will lead with Flora, you will be behind me, and Aunt Lena will be last. When we get up to the front of the line, I will do all the speaking for the family. Do you understand?" Traian accepted his mother's instructions with little emotion. Johanna was aggressively taking charge, and Traian took some comfort and security in her assertiveness.

When they approached the head of the line, they saw that three men sat behind a table with stacks of paper. Johanna handed her passports to the man in the center. He then handed them to the interpreter, who was seated to his right.

"Do you speak Romanian?" the interpreter asked.

"Yes," Johanna replied.

By this time, the man in the center had found Johanna's name on the passenger list and had handed the paper to the interpreter while saying a few words to him in English. At this moment, Johanna became uneasy since she did not understand what was being said. Nevertheless, she fought to retain her outward composure as the process continued.

"Your name is Johanna? These are your children, and the lady in the back is your sister?" asked the interpreter.

"Yes," Johanna replied.

"Why are you coming to America?"

"To live with my husband."

"How long has he been here?"

"About a year."

The questions so far did not bother Johanna, but she was bothered by the penetrating look that was given to her, her children, and her sister by the man at the center of the table.

"Are you or anyone in your family sick?" asked the interpreter.

"No."

"How was the voyage?"

"Good."

Johanna did not want to tell him about her being seasick at the beginning of the voyage. It was none of his business. For the most part, it had been a pleasant journey for her. She had enjoyed the ladies' sitting room, and the food had been good.

After the last question, the interpreter handed the sheet from the passenger list back to the man in the center, who said to Johanna, "That will be all."

Johanna's apprehension was abated. She sighed with relief as she gathered her family and headed for the dining room.

The following morning was the day that all the family had been waiting for. They were to leave the ship. After breakfast, they returned to their stateroom, picked up their packed suitcases, went up to the promenade deck, and joined the line of third-class passengers. They were waiting to leave the ship as soon as it docked alongside its designated pier in New York Harbor. Then first-class passengers proceeded to stream down the gangway while the immigrants in second and third class waited their turn.

After about twenty minutes, these passengers disembarked but were detained on the pier while they awaited the ferry that would take them to Ellis Island. During this time, they formed a line. All the immigrants were given a large tag to attach to the front of their garments. The tag was color-coded to indicate the steamship line, the passenger's manifest number, the name of the steamship, and the passenger's name.

Before she could ask, Traian read what was written on the tag to his mother. Johanna thanked him for the information, however, she still wanted to show him that she was the boss. To assert her authority as she had with the boarding officials the day before, Johanna joined the line of people who were waiting to board the ferry. Flora and Traian followed her, with Lena bringing up the rear.

By that time, the ferry was alongside the pier and a gangway was being positioned for the immigrants who were waiting to board it. Traian begged his mother to move as quickly as possible toward the gangway so that they would be among the first to board the ferry.

The vessel they were about to board was a little over one hundred feet long. It had two covered decks for passengers and an open top deck with lifeboats and a pilot house. The ferry accommodated about three hundred passengers, who were standing and crammed together.

Immediately after the family boarded, Traian darted from his place in line and secured a spot on the front railing of the ferry where he could observe what was ahead. Grabbing Flora, Johanna ran closely behind him, knowing that Lena would follow. When she caught up with Traian, she grabbed him by the shoulder, shook him, and angrily said, "Don't you ever do that again!"

Traian did not respond. At least she hadn't slapped his face. The vantage point that he had secured was worth the punishment. Lena joined them. The family had a very good observation point as the ferry left the pier and headed toward Ellis Island, which was clearly in view. The Statue of Liberty was a half mile beyond it. Johanna, who was no longer angry, was now glad that Traian had taken the action that he had.

As the ferry left the pier, Traian could see the main immigration building. It had red brick walls, large arched windows that were trimmed in limestone, and a tower in each corner that was capped with a green metal dome. To Traian, it was like a castle, and he hoped that he would be able to see the inside. Beyond Ellis Island and its castle-like building, Traian could see the green statue of the woman standing on a square tower.

As the ferry approached Ellis Island, it turned into the waterway that separated the main immigration building from the hospital. Then it headed toward the ferry house, which was situated on a strip of ground that connected the two islands.

From his vantage point at the front of the ferry, Traian was able to see the front of the main immigration building and its portico extending out from the entrance. The ferry house, where they were headed, was an open, large square wooden structure with a pyramidal roof capped with a large cupola. Extending on each side from this large wooden structure were two long wings with lower sloping roofs.

Being among the first to leave the ferry, Johanna was immediately faced with the "groupers." These people shouted while directing the immigrants into two lines: one for men and one for women and children. Johanna and her family found themselves near the front of the women's line. They anxiously awaited what was to come.

The people in the lines that started from the larger building where the ferry had docked were directed toward the main immigration building through the building extension. When they made the turn toward the main immigration building, two doctors were posted there to observe the immigrants from three angles: front, profile, and rear. This gave the doctors the opportunity to scrutinize the immigrants' gaits, postures, and mannerisms.

In an instant, the doctor took in each immigrant's face, skin, hair, neck, hands, and fingers for any signs of disease or deformity. They looked for blemishes, discolorations, and rashes on the skin, nervous twitches, an unusually pale or flushed complexion, profuse sweating, or anything else that might indicate ill health. If any of these signs were visible to these doctors, the immigrant was conspicuously marked on the front of his garment with a large chalk-written letter.

B for back

Ct for trachoma

E for eyes

F for face

H for heart

K for hernia

L for legs

Pg for pregnant

S for senile

X for mental problems.

The immigrants who received these marks stayed in line.

Along the slow moving line, a second set of examiners were posted. Their purpose was to examine the eyes of each immigrant by rolling back the eyelid with a button hook and looking for the telltale scabs of trachoma, a highly contagious disease that often leads to blindness. These examiners were known as the "eyemen." They also looked for signs of other diseases, such as conjunctivitis or cataracts.

The immigrants that were chalk-marked stayed in line. The final determination of their status was to be made by the inspecting officer on the second floor of the main building. Assisted by a doctor and an interpreter, he would make the final determination: admit or detain. The detained immigrants were ushered to the third floor, where women and children occupied one dormitory on the east side of the building and the men were detained in the dormitory on the west side of the building. After more extensive physical examinations were performed, a determination was made as to whether or not the immigrant should be deported or admitted after further treatment and hospitalization.

As they slowly moved eastward on the covered walkway, Johanna noticed a group of men waiting where the line turned south toward the main building. She saw another man selecting an occasional person in line and marking his or her clothes with chalk. Her instincts told her that this should be avoided, and she instructed Traian and Flora to perk up, smile, and walk more briskly.

The family passed the men with a lively cadence, and no chalk marks were received. Johanna was relieved. Traian, on the other hand, was not aware of his mother's continued apprehension, which had been triggered by her unpleasant memories of Chiriac's physical examination in Sânnicolau Mare.

Shortly after making the turn eastward toward the main building, Johanna was stopped by another immigrant officer. He was one of several along the line who was performing eye examinations. Johanna was not as concerned as she had been by the chalking. Everyone in the line was undergoing the examination, which Johanna noticed was uncomfortable and slightly painful.

She offered herself as the first in her family to receive the curling-of-the-eyelid-over-the-buttonhook procedure by the eye examiner. Immediately after her examination, she called for Lena to receive the next exam. Then Traian went, and it was finally Flora's turn. Johanna wanted to shield Flora from any undue anxiety by letting her observe the procedure three times before having to experience it herself.

When it was Flora's turn, Johanna picked her up and held her in her arms. Flora looked up at the eyeman in his uniform: a leather belt and a diagonal strap across the short coat and a policeman's cap, which had a shiny bill.

"Now this won't take long, honey," the eyeman said in a kind voice. Flora did not understand his English comment, but she did see the compassionate look in his eyes as he rolled back Flora's eyelids on the buttonhook. In spite of the eyeman's effort to be as gentle as possible, Flora screamed at the short, unavoidable pain.

The eyeman patted the crying Flora and tried to console her in words that Flora could understand. Johanna was not only surprised but was impressed by the behavior of the eyeman. She wondered if he might have a daughter at home like Flora. Her memory flashed back to Sânnicolau Mare where the treatment of Chiriac was so different. Her eyes teared up as she thought of Chiriac. How was he doing? Would she ever see him again?

After the eye examination, Johanna lined the family up as she had at the beginning, with herself in the lead followed by Traian, Flora, and Lena. The ambling group continued its way out of the open-roofed east wing of the ferry building and moved southward toward the main immigration building along an uncovered walk.

Traian's excitement increased as he impatiently waited to see inside. As they approached the north entrance at the side of the building, they were greeted again by the "groupers," whose job it was to group immigrants from different ships into a specific line for each ship as the immigrants entered the main building. They barked their commands in different languages and shoved immigrants into their proper lines after reading the identification tags on the fronts of their garments.

Johanna noticed that the behavior of these groupers showed undue impatience when they found immigrants in the wrong lines and grabbed and shoved them into their proper lines while openly exhibiting anger and disdain for the bewildered and confused people under their charge. Johanna's gratefulness for the eye examiner's empathy was suddenly erased by the behavior of these groupers. Her uncertainty of what lay ahead suddenly came back while she bit her lip and gathered her determination to meet the next encounter.

The line of immigrants from the *Carpathia* entered the main building from the north entrance and were directed by the shouting groupers to continue down the wide hall to the stairs at the end, which led to the second floor. When they reached the second floor, Traian was overwhelmed by the huge room, which was over two hundred feet long and one hundred feet wide.

A balcony, supported by massive square columns, surrounded the perimeter of the room. The room was flooded with natural light from eight large semicircular windows. There was one window at each end and three along each side. The entire space was covered by a vaulted ceiling, which reflected natural light to the floor below from large beige-colored, glazed bricks set in a herringbone pattern. Traian could not take his eyes off all the spectacular architectural details that dominated the space above.

At the far end of the room were four tables. Behind each table were seated four men interviewing immigrant families. Immigrants that had chalk marks on their garments from the line inspection were examined more closely by a doctor—one of the men seated at the table. Occasionally, someone would be taken out of the line for further inspection. The immigrants were corralled into four lines, which ran along the length of the building between steel railings spaced five feet apart. Each aisle had a continuous bench that was positioned along the railing, which allowed the exhausted immigrants to sit while awaiting their turns to be interviewed.

Johanna, anxious to see what was going on ahead of her, occasionally stood on the bench for a better view of the inspectors' actions. She noticed that immigrants with chalk marks were immediately given a close examination. She also noticed that occasionally, one of the chalk-marked immigrants was separated from the group and ushered up the stairwell at the end of the building. The women were separated from the men and were ushered to the floor above by a matron. The sight of the women being separated from their families gave Johanna a great deal of concern. What would she do if any of her family was sent to the floor above? The uncertainty made her feel very insecure as she anxiously waited for her family to reach the front of the line.

When that finally happened, she mustered up her courage and in a spirited manner, grabbed Traian and Flora by the hand and approached the interview table with an engaging smile while Lena followed behind bringing the luggage. The inspector sitting in the center returned the smile and noticed the tag placed on her blouse showing that she was a *Carpathia* passenger who spoke Romanian. He nodded to the Romanian interpreter at his right, said, "Go ahead," and prepared to make entries in the form on the table.

"Good day, madam," said the interpreter.

"Good day," replied Johanna, who, at the moment, had her eyes on the doctor who was sitting at the right side of the table. When she saw that he did not have a concerned expression while looking her family over, Johanna became more relaxed.

The interpreter asked the usual questions. The answers were entered into the manifest form by the inspector in the center. This involved full names, ages, sexes, marital statuses, occupations, degrees of literacy, nationalities, races, last permanent addresses, and the final destination in America of all family members. Johanna answered each question in a clear and confident voice while the interpreter related her answers in English to the inspector with the manifest list.

After the questioning was completed, the interpreter told Johanna that they would be directed to a ferry that would take them to the rail terminal in New Jersey. Then they would be placed aboard a train to St. Louis. Johanna breathed a sigh of relief but still had some concerns that needed to be addressed with the assistance of the interpreter.

"It's late afternoon, and my family has had nothing to eat since breakfast on the ship. Where can we get something to eat?"

"There is a concession stand downstairs where you can buy sandwiches and something to drink."

"What kind of money will I need?" asked Johanna.

"American money."

"Where can I change my kronen for dollars?"

"There is a money exchange on this floor right behind the stairwell."

Johanna thanked the interpreter and led her family behind the stairwell. There she found a long line of immigrants, which snaked around the room and ended at the cashier stationed behind a wire mesh partition. When Johanna reached the cashier, she counted out the 180 kronen she had remaining in her purse and handed it to the cashier, who counted it and then handed thirty-six dollars back to her.

Although Johanna was illiterate, she was intelligent and could count money. This was the result of her bartering at fairs in Sânnicolau Mare. She counted the thirty-six dollars and put them in her purse. She felt proud knowing that she had six dollars more than Ioan had predicted she should have when she left Ellis Island.

While maintaining control of the family members, Johanna led them downstairs and found the concession stand with a large sign that had, "FOOD FOR SALE HERE," printed in English on it. Below this, there were signs with smaller letters that read:

SMALL PACKAGES $.50
LARGE PACKAGES $1.00
CONTENTS SHOWN IN GLASS CASE

The smaller signs were repeated in ten different languages. After reviewing the smaller signs and the glass cases, Johanna's sixth sense told her that the smaller signs were for the convenience of the immigrants and were printed in different languages. She understood what "$.50" and "$1.00" meant. She grabbed Traian by the shoulder, and while pointing to the smaller signs, she asked, "Are any of these signs in Romanian?"

Traian quickly scanned the smaller signs several times with a puzzled look. After about thirty seconds, he responded in a low apologetic tone. "No, Momma."

Johanna, although disappointed with Traian's answer, was not going to give up. She was the only one who was in a position to see that her family was fed. The numbers shown on the signs were affordable. What she needed was someone who could speak both Romanian and English to help her. Where could she find someone like this? That person might be in the crowded room. She took a deep breath and while standing on her tiptoes, shouted, "Is there anyone in this room who speaks Romanian and English?"

The murmur of voices was suddenly reduced considerably as many in the crowd turned their attention toward the small woman who had shouted something in a foreign tongue. Taking advantage of the reduced background noise and the attention that she had attracted, Johanna shouted once again, "Is there anyone here that speaks Romanian and English? I need help buying food for my family."

After her second shouted request, the crowd became almost silent. Most of the immigrants who were not Romanians stared at her as if they thought Johanna might be mentally disturbed. Those who were Romanians but could not speak English looked at her with pity and were sorry that they were unable to help. Johanna, with increased resolve and determination, shouted her request to the crowd a third time. This time, there was an answer. "Can I help you, madam?" A Romanian interpreter had just come into the concession area.

The interpreter was very polite as he helped Johanna with the purchase of a large package, which contained four sandwiches and four apples for one dollar. He also showed Johanna where a public drinking fountain was located, which spared her the cost of purchasing drinks. Traian's embarrassment from his mother's shouting for help was suddenly transformed into gratitude.

Not only did the interpreter assist in the purchase of a meal but also offered to chat with them while the family sat on the bench in the hall outside the concession room. The interpreter was on his dinner break. In a kind manner, he offered to answer any additional questions that they might have.

Johanna took advantage of the offer. She shared her concern about making contact with Ioan in St. Louis. She wanted to let him know when their train would arrive in St. Louis. This way, Ioan could meet the family at the station in St. Louis. The interpreter told her how a telegram could be sent directly to Ioan from Ellis Island, giving the information.

"How much will that cost?" she asked.

"That depends on the number of words you use. For the information you would be sending, it should cost no more than one dollar," the interpreter answered. Seeing that she had six dollars to spare, Johanna agreed to have the telegram sent.

"The telegraph office is just down the hall. I will take you there and show you how to send a telegram," the interpreter offered.

"Take Traian with you. It will be a good experience for him to learn how to send a telegram," Johanna said as she pushed Traian forward. Johanna reached into her purse and handed a dollar to Traian. She did not want to be placed in a position where she needed to reveal that she could not read or write.

"Have him bring the railroad tickets with him," said the interpreter. "We will need to stop by the railroad ticket office to get the schedule before we send the telegram. I'll bring Traian back here when we are through."

Johanna nodded without speaking, indicating that she understood. She sat back on the bench next to Flora and Lena. Johanna was overcome with feelings of both pride and confidence. Her assertive requests for help had resulted in assistance far beyond her expectations.

After confirming the correct departure and arrival times at the railroad ticket office, the interpreter led Traian to the telegraph office. "Oh hell," he exclaimed in Romanian, "I forgot to get your father's address for the telegram."

"Do not worry," Traian responded. "I have it memorized from the letters I have written to him."

"Smart kid." The interpreter patted Traian on the head as he sighed in relief. With a little help from the interpreter, Traian composed the following telegram using as few words as possible:

Father, leaving New Jersey 9:00 p.m. March 27, arriving St. Louis 8:00 a.m. March 29. Meet us at station. Traian.

The cost of the telegram was seventy-five cents, leaving Traian a quarter, which he proudly handed to his mother after overcoming the temptation to keep it.

At 7:30 p.m., Johanna's family was aboard a ferry from Ellis Island going to the railroad terminal in New Jersey. There were several groupers on the ferry checking train tickets to assure that each person would be boarding the right train.

After leaving the ferry, Johanna could see what the groupers were doing and approached one with her train tickets held visibly in her waving left hand. The grouper scanned the tickets and directed Johanna and her family to one of the half-dozen trains whose cars were backed up to the large area where immigrants were milling around the shouting groupers.

"Here's your train to St. Louis," the grouper said in English, pointing to the last car of the train. Johanna only understood the words "St. Louis," but that was enough to make her confident that she would be boarding the right train. She followed the line of immigrants who were being directed toward the immigrant-coach cars, which were located toward the front of the train, by porters checking train tickets at each car entrance. Eventually, they came to a porter who allowed them to enter their assigned car.

Leading her family into the car, Johanna found two pairs of empty seats across the aisle from each other. She told Lena and Flora to take one pair of seats. Traian claimed the window seat of the adjacent pair. Johanna was about to scold Traian for his selfish behavior but decided it was not worth the effort. With the help of Lena, she put the suitcases in the luggage racks and then sat down exhausted next to Traian. It had been a long and stressful day.

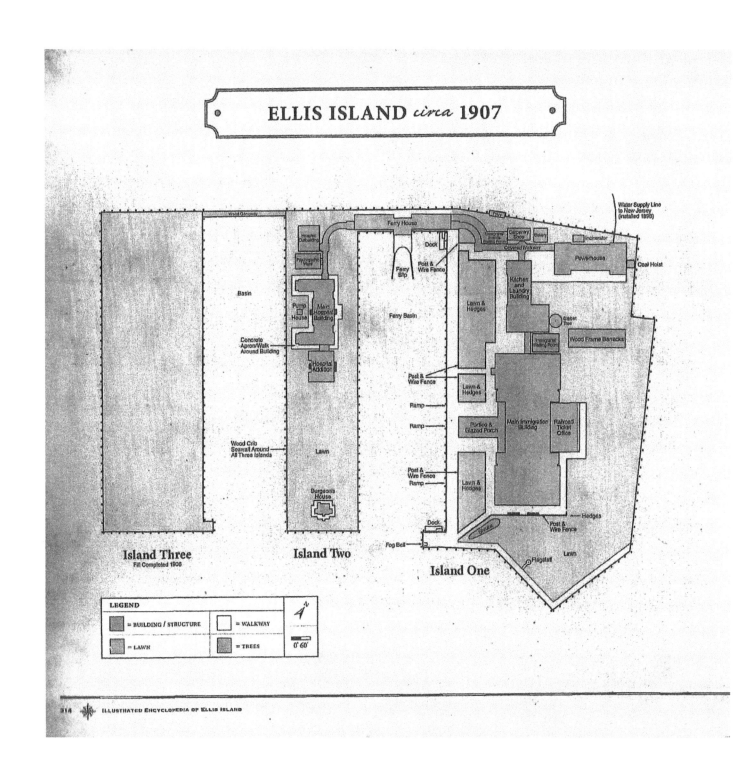

ELLIS ISLAND *circa* 1907

Island Three
Fill Completed 1906

Island Two

Island One

Basin

Ferry Basin

Lawn

Lawn & Hedges

Lawn & Hedges

Lawn & Hedges

Lawn

Hedges

Ferry House

Ferry Slip

Dock

Post & Wire Fence

Covered Walkway

Carpenter Shop

Powerhouse

Coal Hoist

Incinerator

Water Supply Line to New Jersey (installed 1890)

Wood Canopy

Hospital Outbuilding

Psychopathic Ward

Pump House

Main Hospital Building

Concrete Apron/Walk Around Building

Hospital Addition

Wood Crib Seawall Around All Three Islands

Surgeons House

Kitchen and Laundry Building

Gabel Tree

Immigrant Waiting Room

Wood Frame Barracks

Post & Wire Fence

Ramp

Ramp

Portico & Glazed Porch

Main Immigration Building

Railroad Ticket Office

Post & Wire Fence

Ramp

Post & Wire Fence

Dock

Fog Bell

Flagstaff

LEGEND

■ = BUILDING / STRUCTURE ☐ = WALKWAY

▨ = LAWN ▦ = TREES

0' 60'

Ferry boat to Ellis Island.

Ferry Boat House

Johanna at line inspection at Ellis Island

Flora receiving eye inspection

Johanna comforting Flora after eye inspection

Main Examination Hall of Ellis Island

Johanna with Examiners at Ellis Island

Johanna and Traian at food concession Ellis Island

CHAPTER 5
ASSIMILATION

It was a thirty-six-hour train trip with major stops at Philadelphia, Pittsburgh, and Chicago. As on the train trip from Sânnicolau Mare to Trieste, Johanna bought sandwiches, cakes, and fruit for her family twice a day. Although the food vendor spoke only English, he did have the food prices clearly marked on the large tray that was secured to his body with a leather strap running behind his neck. With each purchase, Johanna counted out the correct amount of money, sparing Traian the embarrassment she had caused on the train to Trieste.

Traian spent most of his time looking out the window as the train sped by plowed fields, wooded areas, and small towns. Occasionally, he got up to stretch his legs and walked to the men's restroom, which was at the end of the car. It was similar to the men's room on the Carpathia but much smaller. It only had one toilet, two urinals, and two washbasins. At the major stops along the way, Traian was disappointed that all he could see was the steel-structured train shelter and passengers leaving and boarding the train.

At 8:30 a.m. on March 27, 1909, the conductor walked through the car and loudly announced, "Next stop, St. Louis in thirty minutes." The only words Johanna and her family understood were "St. Louis." The magic words filled them all with such elation that the exhaustion of the long train trip was replaced with energy and invigoration as they approached the end of their three-week journey.

Johanna was concerned with the question of whether Ioan received Traian's message to meet them at the station or not. What would they do if he was not there? After sharing her concern with Traian, she was slightly relieved when he told her that he had his father's address and would find a way to get the family to that location with a cab from the station.

At 8:50 a.m., the train backed slowly into Union Station on one of the twenty tracks that led to the spacious waiting room. As they left the car, Johanna's concern returned. "Where is Ioan? I don't see him?" she called to Traian.

"He probably is in the waiting room at the end of the track," replied Traian, trying to conceal his own concern. After the long walk to the end of the track, they passed through the decorative iron gate and into the large waiting room. There was still no Ioan. Johanna was again overcome with concern as she turned to Traian. She was about to ask him to find a cab when she heard a voice coming from the stairs that led to the street above.

"Johanna? Johanna?" It was Ioan running to greet his family, which he had not seen for a year.

"Ioan! Ioan!" screamed Johanna, running toward him with tears in her eyes and leaving her family with the luggage behind. After a discreet hug and kiss that was appropriate for public display, Ioan and Johanna walked hand in hand across the wide waiting room to greet Lena, Flora, and Traian with the expected hugs and kisses.

"I will now take all of you to your new home," Ioan said as he picked up two of the suitcases and motioned to Traian to pick up the other two. As the family went from the waiting room to the stairs that led to Market Street, Traian could not help but look up at the high-vaulted ceiling over the station's first floor. It was similar to the one he had seen at Ellis Island.

<hr />

At the corner of Market and Eighteenth Streets, they boarded a trolley car headed west toward Grand Avenue, where Ioan and his family got off. From there, they boarded a Grand Avenue trolley, which headed south across Chouteau Avenue and then to LaSalle Street, where Ioan had his family got off the trolley. "It's only a short walk from here," said Ioan.

Together they walked a block west and then past three houses to their final destination. Ioan stopped and pointed to the modest dwelling on the north side of the street. "Here we are," said Ioan proudly as he led his family up the front steps. The porch stretched along the entire front of the house. The house was twenty-four feet wide on a forty-foot lot.

The house had five rooms: a small bathroom, a kitchen, a living room, and two small bedrooms. The kitchen and bathroom had running water. There was a full basement with an enclosed inside staircase from the kitchen. In the basement, there was a large gravity-flow coal furnace with a coal bin. The basement also had four windows. A twelve-foot-wide driveway ran along the left side of the house. The floors were made of pine and were covered with linoleum.

The bathroom had a washbasin with cold water only. There was no tub or toilet in it. Ioan was planning to have them installed after he had enough money saved for it. Until then, the family had to use the privy in the backyard. For the most part, the house was sufficiently supplied with secondhand furnishings that Ioan had been able to obtain over a period of two months before his family's arrival.

The kitchen had a wooden icebox, a large coal-burning cooking range with two ovens, a tall utility cabinet with a chinaware service for six, pewter cookware, and an enameled cast-iron sink with a drain board. In the center of the room was a large table with six chairs.

Each bedroom was furnished with a double bed. Each bed had coil springs, a mattress, two sheets, two blankets, and two pillows. There were no bedspreads. He had also been able to find a chest of drawers for each bedroom but no wardrobes. At the time the house had been built, it had been a common practice not to waste valuable floor space with closets but to use wardrobes to hang garments in. Since he had not been able to afford wardrobes at that time, Ioan had placed coat hooks on the inside part of the two doors leading to each bedroom; one on the door from the bathroom corridor, and one from each adjacent living space to hang garments on.

In the basement, there were two large galvanized-steel round tubs, which were to be brought upstairs for Saturday night baths and Monday's washing. Hot water for these functions would be provided by the kitchen stove as was done in Romania.

The living room was furnished with a large sofa bed, two upholstered chairs, and two end tables with kerosene lamps. A kerosene lamp was also placed in the kitchen and in each bedroom. Windows were covered with roller shades and lace curtains, which Ioan had bought new from a nearby dry goods store with the help of Bucur's wife. It was his hope that this feminine touch would make up for the otherwise drab appearance of Johanna's new home in America.

Not knowing what to expect, Johanna walked into the living room from the front porch. She was immediately drawn to the delicate lace curtains that covered the three windows. The windows provided a generous amount of natural light for the living room. Johanna went to one of the windows and took the lace curtain's hem between her thumb and forefinger with a puzzled look on her face.

"It was made by a weaving machine here in America," said Ioan as he came alongside Johanna. Johanna did not respond. Her thoughts were back in Romania. She pictured the amount of time it took for a Romanian girl to create enough lace just to trim a blouse. Her attention was then drawn to the roller shade behind the lace curtain. She touched it and had the same puzzled look she had shown when examining the lace curtain. She had never seen anything like it in Romania.

Sensing her curiosity, Ioan grabbed the edge of the roller shade, pulled it down a few inches, and allowed the spring roller to raise the shade to a level where it was only a few inches below the top of the window. "This will block the hot summer sun and unwanted eyes from people outside," Ioan said as he pulled the shade down to its original position at the bottom of the window.

Having broken the ice when Johanna apparently accepted their new home by her curiosity at the window, Ioan proceeded to show his family the remainder of their home with a certain confidence and pride. A considerable amount of time was spent in the kitchen. Ioan proudly opened the utility cabinet and pointed out the dishes and mixing bowls in the upper part of the cabinet, the tableware and utensils in the middle drawer, and the pots and pans on the left side of the lower section.

Ioan had stored flour, sugar, and rice in metal containers, several loaves of bread, and a jar of plum preserves. Johanna's spirit rose at the sight of the contents in the utility cabinet as she began to picture herself cooking for her family.

"What is this?" she asked Ioan, pointing to the large wooden object that sat near the wall that separated the kitchen from the stairs to the basement.

"It's an ice box that will keep your meat, milk, cheese, and eggs fresh for a few days, before you cook or eat them," said Ioan. He then showed her where the ice would be placed, the drip pan that Traian was to empty each day, and the card for the iceman. The iceman made his rounds in a horse-drawn wagon, which had blocks of ice that were covered with insulating canvas blankets. The card was about fourteen inches by fourteen inches. The card had large bold numbers along its edge: "25," "50," "75," and, "100."

"When you need ice," Ioan said, "just place it in the front window so that the number of pounds of ice you need is at the top of the card. That way the ice man will know that you need ice and how much he should bring in."

Johanna, noticing a half-empty milk bottle in the icebox, asked, "Where did this come from?"

"We can get it from the grocery store a few blocks away, or for a little more money, we can have it delivered to the front door. We will not need to milk a cow or goat anymore" Ioan proudly replied.

After showing his family the kitchen, Ioan took them downstairs to the basement. It was dimly lit with natural light that came from the four small basement windows. He showed them the furnace, which had a small coal fire burning because of the unusually cold day.

He took a shovel, banked the hot coals to one side, and placed a shovel of fresh coal in the middle of the grate while saying to Traian, "Watch how I am doing this. Never put fresh coal on top of burning coal. It will burn too fast. It will be your job to keep the furnace lit on cold days."

Ioan then opened the door below the hot coals, scooped a shovel full of ashes from the small chamber, and placed it in a basket nearby. "Also, each time you feed coal into the furnace, remove the ashes from below. There are some old newspapers and kindling next to the basket of ashes. The next time we need to light the furnace, I will show you how to do it."

Traian looked at the central-heat gravity-flow furnace that his father was enthusiastically showing him. Above the fire chamber was a sheet-metal bonnet. Large round ducts spread out from it and went to floor registers in each room above. A large twenty-four inch wide return air duct was connected to the bottom of the sheet metal enclosure of the fire chamber. The return air duct was connected to a large register set in the floor above near the center of the house. The air moved up to the bonnet above the fire chamber and then into the hot air ducts that served the room floor registers. Ioan was proud of the new device that had replaced the potbellied coal stoves, which had been in each room and had only been a single source of heat.

From the basement, they went out to the backyard and then to the alley where Ioan showed Traian the ash pile where he was to take the ashes from the basement when the basket was full. Pointing to the privy at the rear of the yard, Ioan said, "In two years, we will be able to afford a toilet and a bathtub inside. Then we won't need this anymore. In the meantime, we will all pretend we are living in Romania."

Johanna reached down and picked up a handful of the rich black soil in the backyard and thought, *This would be a good place for a vegetable garden*. She also wondered if it might not be wise to keep a few chickens, goats, and even a cow in the backyard, which was enclosed with a fence. *The milk from the goats and cows would save us money*, Johanna thought.

After showing the backyard to his family members, Ioan brought them inside to show them the bedrooms. "Flora and Lena will have this bedroom," he said as he opened the door to the back bedroom. "Traian will sleep on the couch bed in the living room." From there, Ioan took them through the small bathroom with only one fixture, the lavatory, and then through the second bathroom door, which led to the front bedroom. Looking at the neatly made bed, Johanna thought of how nice it would be to feel Ioan's warm body next to hers again as they drifted off to sleep.

Johanna found it difficult to find her place in America when she attempted to become more than a hardworking peasant woman. She strived to be a good wife. Her first responsibility was to please her husband and to nurture her children. This was very easy to do without learning how to speak a new language fluently. She did not need it to cook Ioan's favorite Romanian dishes, to tend the vegetable garden, or to encourage Flora to learn how to embroider. As a result, Johanna never learned much English beyond the most common nouns and verbs that were necessary to make purchases at the grocery store.

Ioan became immediately aware of Johanna's hesitance to move too far away from her roots and found himself and the children speaking only Romanian within their home. It seemed to give Johanna more comfort as she tried to find her place in America.

The neighborhood in which they lived was primarily an Irish community, so Johanna was not able to make any new women friends because of the language barrier. The only time she was able to have a conversation with another woman was at church services, which were held each Sunday at Bucur's "place," or at the Romanian festivals, which were held several times a year in the public park. Johanna eagerly looked forward to these occasions when she put on the bright peasant outfit and special shoes that she had brought from Beba Veche. She danced the same dances and sang the same songs that she did back in the old country.

Ioan, on the other hand, felt it was important for his children to learn to speak correct English as soon as possible. He arranged for Flora and Traian to be enrolled in the elementary school that was close to their home.

To help his family adjust, Ioan was able to take the seven vacation days that he had earned so that he could be with his family during their first week in America. On the second morning after their arrival, Ioan took Flora and Traian to their new school. This parochial school had been established by a local church whose congregation was composed of German immigrants. All subjects were taught in English, except religion. Then German was used. It was taught from a catechism printed in German. Because he had been in America for a year, Ioan was able to read and write English well enough to assist Flora and Traian with the new language while helping them with their homework.

After a year in America, Ioan saw that with frugal living, he was able to save more money than he had expected. He dreamed that he might someday return to Romania, buy a nice home, live in luxury for the rest of his life, and not be a burden to his children when he was old. With each paycheck, he was able to put away a little money for his old age while he advanced in his responsibilities at his places of employment.

Several years after his arrival in America, Ioan passed the test required for US citizenship. During his preparation for the test, he learned with great interest, how local, state, and federal government was organized. He was immediately able to see the power of the lower-classed voter. He could use political donations as a means for future favors. He made it a point to read as much as possible about candidates. He made donations to what he thought was the favored candidate. When the odds seemed even, he gave equal amounts to each competing candidate. Ioan no longer was the helpless peasant looking for hope from Nicolae Iorga.

Lena, who was a little more outgoing than Johanna was, knew that living with her sister and her family was a temporary arrangement. She saw that her future lay in being a good wife and homemaker to one of the single Romanian men who attended the church services at Bucur's place each Sunday. After several months of looking the field over, she felt that Cornelius, a man who was slightly older than she was, would be her best choice and began spending more time speaking to him each Sunday after services. In a discreet and slightly flirtatious manner, she exhibited the best qualities a young peasant woman had to offer to an eligible Romanian man. Within a year, Lena married Cornelius and had a home of her own.

Flora was a bright student who mastered the English language as quickly as her father did. Although she did disappoint her mother by not learning to embroider flowers on pillowcases, she made up for it by helping to tend the vegetable garden and with the cooking, after Lena had left. She had a close bond with Traian, who carefully looked after her on the school playground during recess periods.

She attended Central High School, beginning as a freshman in 1915 when Traian started his junior year. She was vivacious and attractive and had her long hair bobbed shortly after high school graduation. This was much to the disappointment of her mother, who found it difficult to think of Flora as anything other than a pretty Romanian maiden with long flowing black hair. To some extent, Flora was a tomboy and enjoyed playing the popular American game of baseball with her older brother and his friends on the Central High School ball field.

Shortly after graduating from high school, Flora began dating a handsome young boy of German descent. Within a year, she was married and moved to Emporia, Kansas, where she raised two children.

Like Flora, Traian found that becoming an American was an easy and natural experience. Like Flora, he learned to speak English quickly. Like his father, he was interested in learning. Science and arithmetic were his favorite subjects. Although he was a little shy, he easily made friends with the Irish boys in his neighborhood, except for the time when he got into an argument with one of them who challenged Traian to a fight. Not wanting to be viewed as a coward in front of his playmates, Traian accepted the challenge, and a scuffle began. It was a hot summer day in August, and as was customary for most boys at that time, Traian was barefoot. His opponent wore shoes and began kicking Traian in the shins. The cheering playmates who were rooting for Traian stopped the contest while one of them took off his shoes and gave them to Traian. Traian put them on and went back to the physical dispute on an equal basis.

There was a saloon in the neighborhood, which was frequented by the fathers of his Irish friends, particularly on Friday, which was payday. At 4:30 p.m., about a half-dozen Irish workmen went into the saloon to reward themselves for a hard week's work with a little libation along with some good old-fashioned socializing. At 6:00 p.m., Traian watched with great amusement as a united band of about six Irish wives entered the saloon and dragged their husbands out before they gave too much of their week's wages to the bartender. He wondered, *What kind of women are these? Momma would never do anything like that.* Traian performed his chores regularly without being reminded. In the winter, he tended the furnace and took out the ashes. When it was time to light a new fire in the furnace, he did it exactly as he had been taught, using no more wood kindling than necessary.

In the attic of their house on LaSalle Street, Ioan built a still for making brandy, which he discreetly sold to trusted customers. Traian's job was to acquire the dried fruit that was necessary to make the illegal beverage. Following Ioan's instructions, Traian would make small purchases of the dried fruit on the same day at several locations. He did this periodically. A large single purchase of this item would arouse suspicion of store owners, who were modestly reimbursed by government agents for revealing this kind of information. To further protect them from suspicion, Ioan had Johanna cook a large batch of sauerkraut and spareribs when the still was running to mask the odor from the illegal operation. This did not bother Traian since sauerkraut and spareribs were one of his favorite dishes.

In high school, Traian showed his athletic ability by becoming a star shortstop on the varsity baseball team. He had a nice write-up on his abilities in one of the issues of the *St. Louis Post-Dispatch*.

In the summer of 1915, Ioan cashed in his chips with a congressman from the St. Louis district. He had him arrange for Traian to go to Washington, DC, and work as a congressional page while living at the Romanian Embassy.

In his last two years of high school during the winter months, Traian spent most of his free time in the gymnasium, where he became proficient on the parallel bars and in gymnastics. He also spent time on the wrestling mat and excelled while competing with others in his weight class. He had a good sense of balance and entertained his gymnastics friends by walking on his hands when going from one place to another, rather than walking on his feet.

After high school, Traian tried out and was accepted for a position on a minor league baseball team, but he decided that it would be better to enroll in the Washington University School of Chemical Engineering. In 1918, he joined the army, three months before the end of World War I. At the end of the war, he was discharged from the army with the rank of corporal.

In each case, assimilation caused the same priorities. First, each person used the immediate means at hand for survival. After basic survival was assured, the next task was building toward the future. In spite of the difficulties, there was always realistic hope.

This hope, in Ioan's case, was fulfilled when he increased his income by being promoted. He did this by overtly demonstrating to his immediate boss that he was laboring more efficiently than his fellow workers were. This was a carryover from making sure that he cut more wheat each day than his fellow peasants in Romania.

Ioan also learned the power of politics with great enthusiasm. From his preparation for his citizenship examination, he saw the difference between the little voice he had by his vote with having no voice whatsoever as a Romanian peasant. Although this was important to him from a general point of view regarding his security, it was also a vehicle for more results in fulfilling his desires. This is when he saw the value of political donations. To him, it was similar to giving bribes to government officials in the old country. The only difference was that in Romania, he knew what favor was expected when the money was given. In America, he considered the money that he gave to be an investment for some future desire he might have.

Modest as they might have been, Ioan always made sure his political donations would be made personally to the candidate so that a memory of his existence would be more easily retained. Ioan considered that his first responsibility was to be the provider for his family. His second responsibility was not to be a burden to his children in his old age.

Johanna, who considered her roles to be that of a wife and a mother, never felt a need for assimilation for survival. She saw that there was no need for her to help Ioan in the same manner as she had in the fields of Romania. Therefore, in her case, assimilation added nothing to improve her role.

Lena considered her assimilation as becoming a wife and raising a family as soon as possible. That became her immediate focus. She followed it like a laser, in a discrete manner, and with all the charm that a young Romanian woman could possess. From the beginning, she knew her choices would be limited. She also knew that all the young men immediately available were quality choices since they all had had the determination to risk leaving the old country to make a better life for themselves. Any one of them would make a good husband as far as she was concerned. It was only a matter of finding the man who would give her the most comfort.

Flora was too young to worry about survival when she came to St. Louis. It was always provided by her nurturing mother as far back as she could remember. It was no different now; it was only happening in a different place. Because of that, assimilation was a comfortable, natural flow of events for her. After she learned the language, which did not take long, her childhood was little different from a child born in America.

In Traian's case, the experience of assimilation was somewhere between Ioan's and Flora's. He had felt a certain responsibility ever since his father had told him that he was the man of the house, the day that his father had kissed him goodbye before boarding the train to Trieste.

The problem had been that he hadn't known what was expected of him in America. He had felt very comfortable and proud of his role while reading his father's mail to his mother when the family had been separated. At such times, it had been clear that he had needed and could provide something that no one else could at that time.

In America, he was uncertain of how to determine what was expected of him in other areas where help might be needed. That uncertainty was immediately abated when his father came back into the picture. His responsibilities were clearly defined by Ioan with assigned chores and high expectations regarding his schoolwork.

In all five cases, there remained a certain attachment to the old country but in different degrees. It was greatest, of course, with Johanna, whose attachment to America was limited mostly to what was necessary for purchasing food for the family. She did not need anything else for her happiness. A cohesive family at meal times, Sunday church services, and an occasional Romanian festival was all that she needed.

Ioan immediately saw the economic value of complete assimilation as soon as possible. He saw that speaking English with an accent was noticed. He worked hard to speak without an accent to avoid discrimination. At the same time, he retained pride in his Romanian heritage and saw to it that his family attended all Romanian church services and festivals.

This pride was greatly stimulated when Queen Marie of Romania visited the United States in 1926 and spent a day in St. Louis. On that day, after a meeting with the mayor and other dignitaries in downtown St. Louis, she attended a special dinner being held in her honor at Washington University by members of the Romanian community in St. Louis.

Ioan was proud to attend this occasion and was able to obtain a seat near the queen, who was seated at the head of the table and on the dais that separated the head table from those of lesser rank like Ioan. On the lapel of his new suit, which Ioan bought for the occasion, was a small Romanian satin flag with broad red, yellow, and blue stripes. Ioan wore it with pride. At that moment, he was fully Romanian in his feelings.

The only problem that he had was how to eat the fried chicken that was being served. Should it be with a knife and a fork, as was done by the more sophisticated, or with one's fingers, as the peasants did? His dilemma was removed when he saw Queen Marie pick up a drumstick with her fingers. His identification as a Romanian became greater than ever.

Family Picture With First Cousins, Circa 1920
Left to Right
Flora, Cousin Joseph, Cousin Dan, Chiriac, Cousin John, Traian

World War I
Seated Right-Traian
Standing To His Left-Bucur

Queen Marie of Romania on
her visit to St. Louis in 1926

CHAPTER 6
CHIRIAC

The next ten years were most productive in Ioan's mind. He started a savings account at the local bank. He saw that payments on a mortgage for a better home would not be much more than the monthly rent that he was paying on the small house where they now lived.

In five years, he saved enough money for a down payment on a bigger house in south St. Louis. It was on the corner of Dresden and Eichelberger and in a more upscale neighborhood. There was a small grocery store (Simons) on the other side of Eichelberger, which was convenient for Johanna. There was also a wooded parkway one block wide and several blocks long (Christi Park) only a block away.

The house had two floors and a basement. There was a large kitchen, dining room, living room, three bedrooms, and a bathroom with a tub, toilet, and lavatory on the main floor.

The house was heated with steam radiators. In the basement, there was a small red coal-fired steam boiler, which was much smaller than the gravity-flow hot-air monstrosity that they had on LaSalle.

The second floor contained a large kitchen, living room, two bedrooms, and a full bathroom with an inside staircase leading to a main vestibule and porch at the backyard. Ioan planned to rent the level above. The rent would offset the mortgage payments, allowing him to pay off the mortgage earlier and save on interest payments, which Ioan hated.

The house had a small front yard, which ran along Dresden Avenue and had a hedge along the sidewalk. In the backyard, there was a garage facing Eichelberger. A concrete sidewalk that lay under a grape arbor connected the house with a side door to the garage.

Ioan was proud of the upgraded living conditions that he was able to provide for his family. With the income from the upstairs apartment, he calculated that he would have the mortgage paid off in less than ten years.

From 1914 to 1916 during World War I, Ioan kept up with the progress of the war through the *St. Louis Post-Dispatch*, which he received daily. Romania remained neutral until 1916 when Romania joined the Allies, France and Great Britain, in their fight against the Central Powers (chiefly Austria-Hungary, Germany, and Bulgaria). As a result, Romania received Banat, Bukovina, and Transylvania, three provinces of Austria-Hungary that had large Romanian populations.

For the first time, Romania's territory included land where large numbers of Romanians lived. Ioan was overjoyed when he read about the final unification of Romanian-speaking people. This had the goal of Nicolae Iorga, who had been Ioan's only hope for a better future when he had lived in Romania.

Liberal political parties now headed the Romanian government. They divided the estates of many wealthy landowners into small farms and sold them to the peasants. Ioan daydreamed about the possibility of going back, buying a small farm, and living out the rest of his life not having to be cared for by his children. But the dream was crowded out by other important tasks that needed immediate attention, one of which was a surprise for Johanna.

In the spring of 1919, a cab pulled up at the front of Ioan's house on Dresden. A sixteen-year-old boy got out of the cab, walked up to the front door, and knocked. It was Saturday. Ioan was sitting in the living room reading. Johanna was in the kitchen preparing dinner with the help of Flora. Traian was in his bedroom studying. At that time, he was a freshman at Washington University and enrolled in the School of Chemical Engineering.

When Ioan opened the door, the boy, without saying a word, reached into his jacket pocket, pulled out a note card, handed it to Ioan, and stared at him with an inquiring look of insecurity while Ioan read the note. It said,

My name is Chiriac. I am from Romania, traveling to America. My destination is 5401 Dresden, St. Louis, Missouri. Please help me get there. I cannot speak English.

This was Ioan's surprise for Johanna. He had been working on it for over a year. He had been corresponding with Father Dimitrie, who had made all the arrangements with the steamship agent for his passport and steamship and train tickets. Their big concern had been whether Chiriac was mature enough to make the trip alone. How could a boy, who was just sixteen years of age and was unable to speak English, be expected to make the journey? Father Dimitrie had wanted to keep the promise that he had made to Johanna when she had learned that she would have to leave Chiriac behind.

Over the years, Father Dimitrie had watched Chiriac grow up. As a boy during World War I, he had been able to avoid the problems of the Hungarian and Bulgarian soldiers, who had passed through Beba Veche on their way to attack Bucharest, by having small portions of bread, sausage, and wine to offer them when they had stopped along the way. Father Dimitrie had noticed that Chiriac seemed to have a sense of survival and appeared to be maturing at an early age.

It may have started with his overcoming the crippling effects of polio and being left behind while the rest of his family had gone to America. Father Dimitrie's reservations had lessened with the encouragement of the steamship agent, who had had a self-serving interest in Chiriac making the trip (his commission). The note had been the agent's idea.

"It should not be a problem from here to New York," the agent had said. "On that part of the trip, he will be with conductors on the train and stewards on the ship. He won't be entirely on his own until he arrives at the train station in St. Louis." That had been when the agent had thought of the note. He had written one note in Romanian and one note in English to be given to the cabdriver at the St. Louis train station. The driver would take him to the proper address.

The tactic of using the note had convinced Father Dimitrie to move ahead. He had allowed Chiriac to travel alone and had shared his confidence with Ioan in his next letter.

Father Dimitrie had been with Chiriac in Sânnicolau Mare when he had passed his physical examination for his passport. He had watched Chiriac's expressions closely as the agent had told him what to expect on the journey to come and how to use the notes the agent had prepared. Chiriac's expressions of curiosity and confidence had been reassuring to Father Dimitrie. His assurance had been reaffirmed when the agent had handed Chiriac the passport and train tickets a few weeks later, just before he had boarded the train to Trieste.

"Now here are your notes. Make sure you don't lose them," the agent had said as he had handed the notes to Chiriac. "The note written in Romanian is for the train conductor on your trip to Trieste and for the stewards on your steamship to America. The note written in English is for the train conductor on your trip to St. Louis."

"I know. You told me the last time I was here. Why are you telling me again? Do you think I am stupid?" Although Father Dimitrie had been a little embarrassed by Chiriac's impertinence, he had been reassured that Chiriac had had the spunk to make the journey alone.

After reading the note and with tears in his eyes, Ioan put his arms around Chiriac while saying in Romanian, "Welcome to your new home, son." Then he turned toward the kitchen and said in a loud voice, "Johanna, come into the living room. I have a surprise for you."

Johanna came into the living room. She wiped her hands on her apron as she stared at the boy standing next to Ioan, just inside the front door. She was puzzled as she slowly approached him. After several seconds, Johanna's maternal instincts triggered her recognition. She screamed out, "Chiriac!" and half fainted on the sofa before she was able to embrace him.

Her scream immediately attracted the attention of Flora and Traian, who came quickly into the living room to see what was going on. Their mother was lying on the couch crying, and Ioan was attending to her and Chiriac, who was standing near the front door with a puzzled look on his face.

Suddenly, they heard another loud knock on the front door. Ioan left Johanna to answer it. It was the cabdriver.

"I just wanted to make sure the kid got to the right place," said the cabdriver. After Ioan assured him that it was the right place, the cabdriver said, "The fare is thirty-five cents."

Ioan handed the driver forty cents while saying, "I will go back to the cab with you and pick up his suitcase."

"He didn't have one," replied the cabdriver.

For his own convenience, Chiriac had thrown away his clothes as they became too dirty to wear. He had left the empty suitcase on the train at Union Station and had arrived at his final destination completely out of clothes and money.

Well, at least he's here, Ioan thought and went back inside.

Johanna had recovered from her shocking surprise. Still drenched in tears, she was hugging and kissing Chiriac. This was followed with a slightly less dramatic but emotional reunion with Traian and Flora while Ioan went to Johanna, who could not completely stop her sobbing.

"Why in the world didn't you tell me he was coming?"

"I wanted to surprise you," Ioan said, grabbing both of Johanna's hands, and looked lovingly into her face.

"Surprise me? You almost killed me with heart failure!" cried Johanna. In anger, she pulled her hands away from Ioan. "I don't know if I can ever forgive you!"

Ioan backed away without any reply or apology. *She will get over it*, he thought. *She's a strong woman.* Johanna's anger with Ioan upset him deep inside, but on the surface, he tried to console himself with a positive attitude. There had been a lot of uncertainty about bringing Chiriac over. He would have to travel alone. What if something happened and he was not able to come? What if he got lost along the way and Johanna never knew what happened?

Ioan had felt deeply sorry for Johanna when he had learned from Traian's letter that Chiriac would not be able to come with the family. But as deep as his sorrow had been, he had assumed that a mother's bond with her child was something so unique that only another mother could fully appreciate it. For this reason, he tried, objectively, to forgive himself for causing Johanna such a shock with his surprise. The brief shock was far better than the lasting grief of losing Chiriac a second time, if for some reason the effort to bring him over failed.

Chiriac's assimilation was easy. He was intelligent and mastered the language quickly. With little effort, he completed high school but had no interest in going to college. Instead, he went from one odd job to another, primarily to have enough spending money to keep up his appearance with nice clothes and to pay his father the token amount of rent that was expected since he was not going to college.

Most of his free time in the evenings was spent in a nearby bar. In spite of his being short, he developed a reputation as being a formidable scrapper after overcoming several challenges from drinkers who thought he would be an easy mark.

It was 1924, and Chiriac was twenty years old. With prohibition on the scene, several prominent gangs in St. Louis indulged in bootlegging, extortion, and robbery. Among them was a gang headed by three Tipton brothers: Herman, Ray, and Roy.

When Al Capone decided to expand his influence in their St. Louis territory, he sent two men to lay the groundwork. The Tipton gang killed them. A short time later, two more men came for the same purpose and were also killed. A third group was sent and met the same fate. The story goes that when Al Capone learned what had happened to his third attempt, he threw up his hands and said, "That's it. I've had it. I'm not messing with these guys anymore. They're crazy, nuts, cuckoo!" From that time on, the Tipton brothers' gang went by the name of the Cuckoo Gang.

In the mid-1920s, the Cuckoo Gang survived a gang war with a rival Sicilian gang called the Green Dragons. Thirteen men were killed on both sides.

Several members of the Cuckoo Gang frequented the bar where Chiriac often went after work. By that time, he was going by the Americanized name of Charlie. In a short time, they and Chiriac began drinking together at the same table. Chiriac knew that his new friends were gang members, but for some reason, it did not bother him.

On one occasion, they invited Chiriac to join their gang. "You will make a lot of money, Charlie," one of them said.

"But will I live long enough to spend it?" was Chiriac's reply, followed by a friendly laugh. He was aware of the recent casualties of the Cuckoo Gang with the Green Dragons. His natural instinct for self-preservation prevented him from making a big mistake.

On the evening of November 16, 1926, Chiriac read an article on the front page of the *St. Louis Post-Dispatch*.

CUCKOO GANGSTER SERIOUSLY SHOT IN FEUD FLAREUP

Louis Mandel Attacked When Riding in His Auto by Several Men in Studebaker Car
FUSILLADE IS FIRED; ASSAILANTS ESCAPE

Victim Does Not Know Who Shot Him or Why, He Says, and Does Not Amplify Story

Another episode in the deadly bootleg feud between Cuckoo gangsters and Italian gunmen occurred at noon today, when a Cuckoo, Louis Mandel, 24 years old, was shot and seriously wounded by several men in a curtained Studebaker touring car who fired a Fusilade into his Ford coupe as they sped past him on Prairie Avenue at Garfield Avenue.

Shot twice in the left arm and once in the left jaw, Mandel lost control of his car and it jumped a curb and crashed against a post. He climbed out and staggered into the corner saloon of Jacob Haberman who called the police to take him to City Hospital.

Assailants had disappeared.

His assailants had disappeared after throwing into the street two revolvers from which 11 shots had been fired. No weapon was found in Mandel's bullet-riddled coupe.

Mandel was driving south on Prairie, he told police, when "some fellows" in the other car, also going south, fired at him, quite to his surprise. He said he did not know who shot him, or why. That was his story, and he was not inclined to amplify it.

Arrested 60 times.

He gave his address as 106 North Fourteenth Street but police say he lives at 3034 Dickson Street. The Fourteenth Street address is a real estate office and a rendezvous of the Cuckoo gangsters. Mandel and eight others were arrested there the night of Oct. 21 by police who found them "just sitting around" in the darkened office, in which there were hidden five pistols and a double-barreled shotgun.

In the last 11 years, Mandel has been arrested 60 times for investigation and on various charges, but never convicted. He is now out on bond on a charge of attempted burglary at the Columbia Theater, 5251 Columbia Avenue.

That could have been me, Chiriac thought after reading the article. Then after a long stretch in his easy chair followed by a yawn, he took the last sip of beer in his glass on the end table and went to bed.

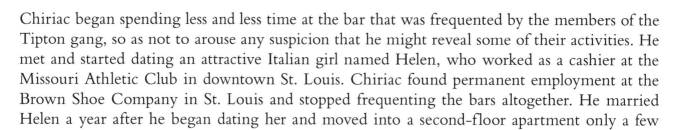

Chiriac began spending less and less time at the bar that was frequented by the members of the Tipton gang, so as not to arouse any suspicion that he might reveal some of their activities. He met and started dating an attractive Italian girl named Helen, who worked as a cashier at the Missouri Athletic Club in downtown St. Louis. Chiriac found permanent employment at the Brown Shoe Company in St. Louis and stopped frequenting the bars altogether. He married Helen a year after he began dating her and moved into a second-floor apartment only a few blocks away from his father's residence.

Married life softened the image that he had created for himself in the bars. He became a favorite of his nephews and nieces, who would become part of his life in the years to come. For them, he was the favorite, Uncle Charlie, who always passed out nickels and dimes to them on family get-togethers so that they could buy ice-cream cones at nearby confectionaries.

He became a Shriner. As one of their clowns, he blew up balloons and twisted them into animals and other objects to amuse the children who were watching him in the parades.

At Christmas, he would don his red-velvet Santa Claus suit and make surprise visits to his young nieces and nephews. He enjoyed being the center of entertainment. He always had new jokes to tell and new riddles to ask. In spite of it all and for the remainder of his life, he retained his reputation for his street smarts and survival.

Elena and Chiriac 1912

Christina and Chiriac

ST. LOUIS POST-DISPATCH

BENEFIT CARNIVAL: Moolah Shrine clown Charles Pistui passing out animal balloons to young admirers at a carnival organized by a group of children in Manchester. Proceeds will go to fight muscular dystrophy. (Post-Dispatch Photo)

CHAPTER 7
THE COURTSHIP

After his discharge from the army in mid-November of 1918, Traian enrolled in the School of Chemical Engineering at Washington University. Because of his late enrollment, he was buried in makeup homework so that he could catch up with his class. With the extra time he had available during his Christmas vacation, he was finally able to catch up.

Shortly after Chiriac arrived, Traian took his younger brother under his wing as Chiriac quickly adjusted to his new life in the United States. Once he became proficient in the new language with the help of Traian, Chiriac quickly shed the role of the needy little brother and asserted his independence.

"I don't need you to tell me what to do anymore. I am seventeen years old now and will do whatever I want," Chiriac said to Traian. It was also a challenge to Ioan, who was in the room when the remark was made. Traian looked at his father for guidance. Ioan said nothing. When Chiriac left the room without saying a word, Ioan stared at Traian and moved his right arm horizontally, indicating that Traian should not make any more waves. From then on, Traian focused only on his schoolwork and left Chiriac's guidance entirely up to Ioan.

＊＊＊

Several months after the incident with Chiriac, Ioan became bedridden with tuberculosis and was no longer able to work. Since there was no health insurance or company health benefits at that time, Ioan was without a paycheck. With the rent from the upstairs apartment and the rent money from Chiriac, which was not always certain, Ioan saw that he did not have enough to meet the mortgage payment along with other expenses. Added to this deficit were the medical expenses that Ioan did not have in his budget.

While Johanna and Flora were cleaning the table after supper one evening, Ioan called Traian to his side. "Well, son, it looks like you are going to be the man of the house again until I get back on my feet." Ioan then showed Traian the notes that he had made when he had calculated the monthly income and expenses for the family and the resulting deficit that needed to be withdrawn from the savings account each month to meet expenses.

"You will have to collect the rent, withdraw the money needed each month from the savings account, and pay the mortgage each month," Ioan said while handing his notes to Traian. Traian looked them over. He was surprised at the amount in the savings account. He did not expect it to be that large.

"Don't worry, Papa," he said, "I will be able to take care of this for you."

In order to reduce the amount that would need to be withdrawn from the savings account, Traian obtained a part-time job. This eliminated his free time, which he usually spent in the gym and required him to burn the midnight oil to keep up with his classwork.

Chiriac was one of Traian's problems. He had been spending more of his free time in the saloon and occasionally came home with scars on his face, indicating that he had been in a fight. One evening while studying late, someone knocked on the door. When Traian answered the door, a young man about his age asked, "Are you John?" (John was the Americanized name that Traian had adopted). "I am a friend of your brother. He was in a fight and was taken to Barnes Hospital."

"Thank you. I will go there right away." Traian sighed deeply as he pondered his next steps. Ioan, Johanna, and Flora were all in bed. He decided to tell only Flora what had happened and where he was going. He would fill her in on the details after he got back from the hospital.

After walking several blocks to Kingshighway Boulevard, Traian boarded the Kingshighway streetcar and went north to Barnes Hospital, which was several miles away. After he checked in at the admitting office, he was given Chiriac's room number and was told that visiting hours were over. Under the circumstances, he would be permitted to see his brother but could only stay a half hour. In those days, hospital visitations were quite limited, making it more convenient for the small staff to care for the patients.

He went up the stairwell to the second floor, stopped at the nurse's station, identified himself to the nurse on duty, and asked, "How bad is he?"

"He has a stab wound on the left side of his abdomen," the nurse replied while looking at his chart. "Twelve stitches. He should be okay if no infection sets in." The nurse then led Traian down the hall to the four-bed ward where Chiriac was sleeping. "If you want to speak with him, I will wake him up. But keep your voices down so you don't wake up the other patients."

Traian stared at Chiriac, who was sleeping soundly, and decided not to wake him up. "I think it's best that we let him sleep. When he wakes up, tell him I was here and will see him tomorrow at 7:00 p.m."

It was 1:00 a.m. when Traian got home. He woke Flora up and told her the extent of Chiriac's injuries. They both decided to tell their parents that Chiriac's injury came from being struck by an automobile while crossing the street. That way, they would worry less.

The next day at 7:00 p.m., Traian entered Chiriac's ward not knowing what to expect regarding his brother's attitude. Chiriac had been making bad choices about the company he had been keeping over the past year and had reacted with anger and defensiveness whenever his father had tried to lead him away from his saloon friends. To Traian's surprise, Chiriac greeted him with a welcome smile. "Hello, big brother," Chiriac said with a cordial look that made Traian feel comfortable about asking what had happened. Chiriac spoke about the encounter in an objective matter-of-fact way. He did not hide or excuse the fact that he had been in many barroom scrapes before. The only difference was that this guy pulled a knife on him.

"Do you know the guy? asked Traian.

"No, he was from another gang," answered Chiriac.

"What do you mean another gang?" Traian responded with a frown.

"You don't want to know," Chiriac replied evasively and without showing any emotion.

Traian decided to take advantage of what appeared to be a softening of Chiriac's overall attitude. "I know it's none of my business," he replied diplomatically, "but why do you get in so many fights?"

"I never start them. They always pick on me."

"Why?" asked Traian.

"I don't know. I guess because I am short and they want to show everyone in the place how tough they are. But don't worry. I can take care of myself," Chiriac replied softly with self-assurance.

"Does this ever happen outside the bar?"

"No."

"Then why don't you stop going to the bar?" Traian said while staring at the floor. His tone was low. He did not want to make Chiriac feel like he was being told what to do. He hoped he would accept the question as a suggestion.

"It wouldn't be a bad idea," replied Chiriac without showing any belligerence to Traian's suggestion. "But it isn't as easy as it sounds."

Traian decided not to pursue the matter any further. At least a respectful communication had been established with his brother without saying anything more to him about the frequency of his visits to the saloon.

Chiriac's instincts for self-preservation began to influence his behavior. He thought, *What would happen if the next fight involved a gun?*

Ioan was still bedridden, so Johanna looked after him. He was weak and coughed constantly. In the afternoon, he usually came down with a fever. She tried to comfort him by bathing his forehead with a cool, damp cloth. The doctor suggested that Ioan go to the tuberculosis sanitarium, but he resisted. Johanna was taking good care of him, and in a few weeks, he thought he would be better.

After two months, he was no better, and Johanna started coughing. Traian noticed that she was moving more slowly and was concerned. More of his time was needed to help his mother. He chose not to sign up for his junior year at Washington University so that he would have more time to help at home. He soon found that this had been a good idea since his mother continued coughing and getting weaker. Ioan, although not getting better, was holding his own.

In the early part of 1921, Johanna also contracted the disease. Traian found himself caring for both of them with help from Flora. He got a full-time job working at the post office to help with expenses while Flora cared for Ioan and Johanna during the day.

In early 1922, Ioan began showing signs of recovery while Johanna began to get worse. Within a few months, Ioan had completely recovered. He began helping Flora take care of Johanna.

By this time, Traian found a little more free time and started going to social events at a place in Madison, Illinois, known as the Romanian Hall. There seemed to be a larger number of Romanian immigrants in Madison. Traian, who was a little on the shy side when it came to young women, felt more at ease with the young Romanian ladies he met at the Romanian Hall.

One in particular was Christina. She had been born in Beba Veche in 1902 and had immigrated with her father, mother, older sister, and younger brother in 1907, two years before Traian had immigrated. Christina had been four years old at the time. Her father was a bit of an entrepreneur. He had a small barbershop between Third and Fourth Streets on Madison Avenue and sold real estate in his spare time.

Traian was immediately attracted to Christina. They had much in common because they had been born and had lived in the same peasant village in Romania. They had lived in homes where Romanian had been the only language used by their parents while at home.

In their conversations, Traian told Christina about his life as a boy in Beba Veche and the voyage to America. Christina, being four years younger, remembered little about that part of her life. She felt a little inferior when Traian started talking about high school and college. Christina had only graduated from elementary school. Her father, Georgio, felt she had had enough education and had told her that she should get a job at the packinghouse near Madison. As was the custom with young immigrant children, Christina had done this without question.

Christina was also attracted to Traian. He was handsome, and he exhibited an image of reliability as he talked about having to quit school to help take care of his parents. She had a certain sense of humor about her and used it in a way to balance their differences in formal education. "You may have a lot of book learning," she once told him, "but do you have any common sense?"

"And how do I get common sense, Teeny?" By that time, Traian was calling Christina "Teeny," which was the Romanian diminutive for Christina.

"From watching animals," she said. "They have learned to survive without reading a single book."

"Do you watch animals?" Traian asked.

"Every day," she said.

"And what did you learn?"

"I thought you would never ask," Christina said with a twinkle in her eye like someone who had just sprung a trap. Then she told Traian about the animals that her parents kept in the backyard of their house on Iowa Street, which was only a few blocks away from Georgio's barbershop. She told Traian that they had chickens, a cow, and several pigs, which Christina said she had to look after.

"Now when I go into the chicken coop with a bucket of feed, they know they are about to be fed and run up to me. When I come in with an empty pan, they know I am going to gather eggs, and they go about their business. But when I come in with nothing in my hands, they know that one of them is about to become supper, and they all run from me."

"And what about the cow?" Traian asked.

"Now, John, the cow was different. When I was in grade school, after school, it was my job to take her down the block to a grazing field for an hour so she could eat her supper. She knew the time that I came home and was always waiting for me at the gate with a rope around her neck that I would use to lead her down the block to the grazing field.

"We were the only family on the block with a cow in the backyard. A young girl leading a cow down the street attracted the attention of my playmates, who usually joined me to keep me company while our cow was grazing. When the grazing time was up, the cow came to me, dragging her rope so that I could lead her home. Once in a while, she would decide she did not want to go home. Instead of coming to me, she would walk into the middle of the shallow pond next to the grazing area."

"What did you do then?" Traian asked with a smile of amusement.

"We then would throw rocks at her. That showed her who was boss. She would come out of the pond and let me lead her home," Christina answered. "You know, John, thinking back, I really hated that job."

"Why?"

"Well," Christina answered with a pensive look," I guess it was because we were the only family in the neighborhood that had a cow. I always felt self-conscious leading her down the street."

"And now, what can I learn from your pigs?" Traian asked with interest and amusement.

"My father would always buy a baby pig each month when they were cheap. He would butcher and eat the oldest one when it was six months old. Like the chickens, they were fed each morning when I brought food scraps to their feeding trough. The oldest one was always kept in a separate part of the pigsty.

"I placed corn in his feeding trough for his final month to fatten him up before butchering. When it was time to butcher the oldest pig and we came to his sty to move him to the butchering area, the pig always seemed to know that the good times were over. He did his best to get away before ending up in the roasting pan.

"I will never forget the time back in early November 1919 when the city of Madison was celebrating Armistice Day with a parade down Madison Avenue. Our family decided to join in the celebration by butchering our oldest pig. As usual, when the pig saw us entering his section of the sty, he became agitated, ran out of the sty before anyone could stop him, and started running toward Madison Avenue where the parade was taking place. He was followed by my father, brother, and three other Romanians. They formed their own parade, which disrupted the city parade. They ran behind the row of baton-twirling drum majorettes and the first row of the band."

This brought a laugh from Traian as he pictured the story Christina had told. She looked amused herself while recalling the incident.

"You know, Teeny, we could make a great team—you with your common sense and me with my book learning."

So the courtship began. It was a typical Romanian courtship. Christina was invited to Sunday dinners that had been prepared by Flora at Traian's house. Johanna, at this time, was still bedridden, but she took an immediate liking to Christina. Johanna's conversations with Christina were on subjects like cooking, housekeeping, sewing, and fancy needlework. Christina demonstrated considerable interest and proficiency in all these. She even brought Johanna samples of her own needlework.

Traian's similar visits to Christina's house on Iowa Street followed the same pattern. This time the talks were between Traian and Christina's father, Georgio. The subject matter was Traian's education, his work, and whether or not he was planning to go back to college after his mother recovered. Traian told Georgio that at this time, he really did not know. It depended on how long it would take for his mother to recover.

While the getting-to-know-each-other process of the courtship had taken place, there had not been any formal proposal. The subject of marriage had been avoided with discretion.

In the fall of 1923, Johanna's condition became steadily worse. She began coughing up blood. She was taken to Barnes Hospital for an x-ray of her lungs to determine how far advanced the disease had become.

To make her as comfortable as possible, Ioan insisted that she be placed in a semi-private room. Johanna did not have a roommate when Ioan and Flora visited her the following morning while Chiriac and Traian were at work. While they were there, Johanna's doctor made his routine visit. Prior to that, he had examined Johanna's lung x-ray, which had been taken the day before. After his bedside examination with a stethoscope and checking Johanna's chart at the foot of her bed, the doctor asked Johanna how she was feeling.

"Not good," Johanna replied. By this time, her understanding of English had improved to the point where she could understand and respond to simple questions. She looked for any facial expression from him that would indicate his real opinion.

"I know," said the doctor. "You are a very sick lady."

Johanna immediately sensed from his reply that her condition was bad. On the way out, the doctor signaled for Ioan to meet him in the corridor. The signal, which was intended to be hidden, was observed by Johanna.

"I am afraid I have some bad news for you," the doctor told Ioan and Flora as they stood in the hall outside Johanna's room.

"How bad is it?" asked Ioan.

"It's terminal," said the doctor.

"How long do you expect her live?" Ioan asked with tears in his eyes.

"Six months. Maybe nine."

The next day, Johanna was back in her home. She knew she was going to die. Between bouts of coughing and naps, she began to think of things she wanted to have happen before she died. The first was that Traian would marry Christina. The second was that Ioan would agree to find himself another good wife after Johanna had passed away. She made these wishes known to both Traian and Ioan repeatedly when she was awake and was able to talk to them.

Ioan reassured her by saying, "Johanna, if I ever find a woman as good as you, I will marry her. I promise."

Although Traian had strong feelings for Christina, he did not want to get married until after he completed college and was able to support her. It took him several days to think it over before assuring his mother that he would begin his plans to marry Christina immediately.

The next time Traian had dinner with Christina and her family, he found time alone with her father and told him that he would like his permission to marry Christina. Georgio told Traian that marriage was a big step in one's life and asked if Traian had thought thoroughly about what he was getting into. After Traian told him that he cared for Christina very much and that he would be a good husband to her, Georgio answered, "I like you, Traian, but when and whom she will marry is up to Christina."

With the first step behind him, Traian found time alone with Christina. With the precision of an engineer on a tight time schedule, he immediately asked Christina to marry him. Christina was stunned. She liked Traian, enjoyed his company, and considered him to be good husband material, but she was not expecting a proposal from him this soon. Also, to her, the proposal seemed more like a quick business decision rather than a carefully planned romantic strategy.

To Traian's disappointment, Christina's answer was, "John, I like you very much. I know you would make a good husband, but I need time to think about this. Let's keep going the way we have been for a while."

Several days after Traian's proposal to Christina, she had dinner with Traian's family. After the meal, Flora suggested that Christina visit with Johanna in the bedroom while she and Traian did the dishes. Johanna was half-asleep at the time and was perspiring because of a low-grade fever. Christina began to bathe her head with a damp cloth from the washbasin that was on top of the chest of drawers next to the bed. Johanna began to wake up.

"Good day, dear heart," Johanna said to Christina in Romanian. "How are you?"

"I am fine. Thank you, Mamma," Christina replied, also in Romanian. Her use of the greeting "Mamma" was intended to be a sign of respect and endearment that Christina often used when addressing older Romanian women.

"When are you and Traian going to get married?" Johanna asked, this time in a stronger voice. She was now wide awake and was looking at Christina with a piercing stare. Christina was again taken by surprise by the sudden mention of marriage. Johanna stared at Christina with a look of impatient disappointment.

Christina felt trapped while she searched for the right answer. "As soon as you are better, Mamma, and can come to the wedding," Christina answered. It seemed strange to her that her commitment to marriage had been made to Johanna before it was made to Traian.

"No, darling. I am dying. I do not have long to live. My wish is that I see you married to Traian before I die. I know you will make him a good wife."

Again, Christina felt trapped. Her pity for Johanna seemed to overcome all of her other emotions. "Don't worry, Mamma. If that is your wish, we will make it happen."

When Traian took her home, Christina told him that they needed to talk. She had him sit next to her on the front porch swing. She told him about her conversation with his mother and Christina's response to the two of them getting married before Traian's mother died.

After hearing this and seeing the look in her eyes—like a person who had been tricked—Traian took both of Christina's hands in his and he softly said, "Teeny, the most important thing to me is this: Do you love me enough to marry me? Can you see yourself being happy living with me and raising our children? Teeny, I love you very much, and I want you to be my wife."

For the first time since the subject of marriage had been brought up, she sensed that her feelings were finally being considered. She accepted the rush to the altar. With the help of her older sister Anna, she picked out a white calf-length wedding dress and a short veil that formed a crown over her head, which was decorated with pearls.

On January 20, 1924, Traian and Christina were married in a morning as the snow blew. After the wedding mass, a reception was held for the wedding party and invited guests. Following the reception, Traian, Christina, and the wedding party went to visit Johanna in two limousines rented by Ioan. After seeing the delight in Johanna's eyes as the wedding party entered her bedroom, Christina was comforted by knowing that she was able to fulfill Johanna's last wish, even though Christina had felt all along that she was being rushed into marriage. For the moment, these feelings found their way into the deeper recesses of her mind.

Johanna died in the summer of 1924. She was buried at Lakewood Park Cemetery, on Mackenzie Road, about two miles southwest of her home on Dresden. Ioan bought a large gray granite headstone topped with a cross to mark her grave.

1923
Standing: Christina, Nick, Anna, Pete
Seated: Persida, Helen, George

George Argelan

JOHANNA AND PERSIDA'S GRAVE STONES
LAKE PARK CEMETARY, ST LOUIS MO

CHAPTER 8
A YOUNG FATHER

While preparing for his marriage to Christina, Traian got a job at the coke plant in Granite City, which was adjacent to the city of Madison. About a mile west of the plant, there was a small neighborhood of affordable houses, which Traian thought were within walking distance from his work.

With the advice of his father, along with a loan for the down payment, he purchased a small residence at 2323 East Twenty-Fourth Street. Its layout was very similar to his first home in St. Louis on LaSalle Avenue. It had a living room, large kitchen, two bedrooms separated by a bath, and a full basement with the same type of gravity-flow furnace. A one-car garage with an adjacent shed was at the end of the backyard next to the alley.

The bathroom had a lavatory with hot and cold running water and a water closet. Like the house on LaSalle, it did not have a bathtub. The weekly baths would need to be taken in washtubs brought up from the basement, just like Johanna had had to do on LaSalle Street.

Late afternoon on March 3, 1925, Christina's water broke, and she began to have labor pains. They called Dr. Reuss, their family doctor, from the next-door neighbor's telephone because Traian did not have a telephone in his monthly budget. Dr. Reuss came in his new 1924 Chevrolet coupe with his nurse. In those days, doctors made house calls. They were often accompanied by their nurses. Most babies were delivered at home.

Late in the evening of March 3, Christina was weak with labor. Dr. Reuss determined that she could not deliver the baby without assistance and decided to help her with the use of forceps, which was common at that time. Shortly after midnight on March 4, 1925, Christina's first baby came into the world. It was a boy. He cried while the nurse wrapped him in a baby blanket. Then she handed the infant child to Christina, who turned tenderly toward the little one who now was quiet and beginning to fall asleep.

Dr. Reuss and his nurse left the house in the middle of a snowstorm, which had started an hour before, and headed across the street toward Dr. Reuss's car. As they approached the center of East Twenty-Fourth Street, a car sped from the north. When the driver saw the two pedestrians a half block ahead of him, he slammed on his brakes, skidded about one hundred feet, and slowed down to a stop after striking Dr. Reuss and his nurse. The driver backed away from the two victims lying in the street, pulled around them, and sped away.

Traian, who was standing on the front porch, observed the entire incident. He ran down to the doctor and his nurse, who were lying in the middle of the street and were still conscious.

Fortunately, the hit-and-run driver's car had been slowed down considerably before hitting the doctor and the nurse. The doctor had a broken ankle. The nurse was badly bruised and scratched up. Traian and the nurse helped Dr. Reuss into the living room. Following that, Traian went to the next-door neighbor's house and the to call an ambulance for the doctor. The ambulance driver's assistant followed the ambulance to the hospital in Dr. Reuss's car.

The new baby was named John, which was the name Ioan and Traian had been using for over twenty years. The baptismal ceremony took place at Sacred Heart Church, which was a small wooden church located at the intersection of August Avenue and Washington Avenue. It was a Catholic church and the nearest thing Traian and Christina could find to a Romanian Orthodox church.

Bucur's son was baby John's godfather at the ceremony. Bucur Jr. had been accepted by his generation of the Romanian community in St. Louis as their quasi leader. He was very active in assisting new Romanian immigrants to get settled in St. Louis. His father and mother had moved back to Romania to retire after selling the tavern and restaurant to Bucur Jr. and his wife before they left. It was the Romanian custom, at that time, that the godfather and the godmother of a child would assume the responsibility of raising that child if his or her father or mother died.

Like all young mothers with their first babies, Christina was both surprised and overwhelmed with the amount of time it took to care for a newborn infant. One afternoon when Traian came home from work, he found Christina at the stove cooking their supper with young Johnny on her hip crying. Traian picked him up and started patting his back hoping to settle him.

Traian asked, "What's wrong with him?"

Christina, thankful to be temporarily relieved of her burden, responded without looking at Traian. "I don't know. He's been crying all day."

"What do you think we should do?" Traian asked.

Christina then turned to Traian, looked him straight in the eye, and said, "I think we should ask Dr. Reuss to come live with us." Seeing Traian's puzzled look, she then smiled and said, "Give him to me. I think he's hungry."

Christina then took the infant from Traian and began nursing him while Traian finished supper with a puzzled, helpless look still on his face and thinking, *It looks like Teeny has been able to keep her sense of humor.*

When Christina had delivered her first child, she had not had her mother's assistance during the first few months of caring for her new baby. At that time, her mother had been sick with tuberculosis. Her mother passed away several months after Johnny was born. Her father purchased a burial plot next to Johanna's grave and had a large red granite headstone, which was similar in size and shape to Johanna's, placed at the head of her grave.

Christina did have help from her older sister Anna, who was also a young mother with a four-year-old daughter, Helen. Anna was married to Nick, who happened to be a first cousin to Traian. Nick was born in Beba Veche in 1913. He immigrated to St. Louis when he was a young man, after spending some time in Vienna learning the barber trade. Nick and Anna lived in the upstairs apartment of Ioan's residence. He had a three-chair barbershop on Bates Street and drove a Model T Ford to work each morning.

During the first few months after Johnny's birth, Anna and Helen would take the Gravois streetcar once a week to downtown St. Louis, where they would transfer to the Illinois Terminal Line to Granite City. It was only a one-mile walk from the last stop at Twenty-Third and State Streets in Granite City to her sister's house. The whole trip took about an hour and a half. Christina was grateful for the extra effort that Anna was making to help her out. They both spoke English to each other in front of Helen. They wanted her to identify herself as an American and to not be teased about coming from an immigrant family. In time, Christina gained confidence in caring for Johnny.

Traian started working in the by-products division of the coke plant. He was an operator. He read gauges and adjusted valves on a complex array of equipment that converted gas from coke ovens into tar, fertilizer, benzene, and natural gas. Traian's chemistry courses from the two years that he had studied at Washington University helped him understand the process. He was soon promoted to foreman, which allowed him to put a little more money in the bank with each paycheck.

A year and four months after her first delivery, Christina gave birth to her second child, another boy. This time the delivery was normal, and there were no unfortunate incidents with the doctor or his nurse. He was christened Bucur to honor his godfather Bucur Jr. but was called Billy. Christina had fewer uncertainties with the second child than the first, although caring for two babies in diapers was time-consuming.

Traian made it a habit to wash diapers the minute he came home from work. A double laundry sink was in the basement where Christina kept the moist diapers that had been rinsed in the upstairs water closet. After scrubbing about a half-dozen diapers on the washboard with a bar of laundry soap, Traian rinsed them, wrung them out by hand, and then hung them on the clothesline in the basement to dry. After several months of this, Traian decided that Teeny needed a new washing machine. At that time, there was a state-of-the-art Maytag washer with an agitator, which was run by an electric motor, and roller wringers, which were electrically operated.

Christina's brother Pete and his wife, Irene, lived several blocks away on Hodges Avenue. They became close friends with Traian and Christina.

Like his father, Pete was an entrepreneur with many skills. After finishing high school, he enrolled in a work/study vocational college in Cincinnati, Ohio, where after a year, he became proficient in carpentry, masonry, plumbing, and wiring. He also became a barber and set up a barbershop in the enclosed sunporch of their home.

Occasionally, Irene would walk to Christina's for a visit and help with the babies. Saturday nights, the two couples often got together for pinochle, cake, and coffee, after the two boys had been put to bed.

Three years after the birth of Billy, Traian and Christina decided that it would be nice to have a girl to complete the family. In the spring of 1930, Christina was pregnant with her third child, which she prayed would be a girl. She chose not to even think of another boy and began telling her two boys that they soon would have a baby sister.

Traian, seeing her deep desire, decided to go along with the idea that it would definitely be a girl when talking to the two boys. At that time, the boys were led to believe that the baby would be delivered by a stork. Traian wondered what he would tell the boys if the new baby turned out to be a brother instead of a sister. Looking ahead, he decided that he would say that the stork had made a mistake and would not take the baby back.

On June 2, Christina went into labor, and Traian took the two boys over to Pete and Irene's house for an overnight stay, which happened often. On the morning of June 3, Traian came to visit his two sons, who were playing with toy soldiers on the living room floor as Irene let Traian in. "Well, boys, your little sister is here," Traian said smiling as the two boys looked up from their toys.

"Great!" Johnny replied with a happy look on his face. "Can we go see her?"

"Not today. Your mother is sick. Maybe you can see your sister tomorrow when Momma's feeling better."

Christina was slightly sedated with chloroform, which made the pain of delivery tolerable while still allowing her to assist as much as naturally possible with the delivery. Traian had arranged to take a few days off from work to care for their baby girl, whom they had named Jane Edith. Edith was the English translation of Christina's mother's name, Persida. A white-painted metal baby crib with a vertically adjustable guardrail was placed in the corner of the back bedroom where the two boys shared a double bed.

After about seven months, Jane was standing up, holding the top of the guardrail, staring, and cooing at her two brothers in the adjacent bed. After having cared for two boys, Christina found that raising her little girl was much easier. Christina was a natural homemaker and mother. She saw her role as one who was responsible for saving as much of her husband's income as possible.

Between cooking, washing, and ironing, she found time to can fresh fruits and vegetables, which Traian had bought by the bushel when they were in season. She was also an excellent seamstress and made her own clothes as well as her children's, using the secondhand treadle-operated Singer sewing machine, which Traian had bought for her shortly after Jane had been born. She had a knack for examining a particular garment that she liked and then cutting out a pattern from old newspapers to make the garment.

From 1924 to 1930, Traian and Christina experienced the prosperity of what was called the Roaring Twenties. The coke plant, blast furnaces, and steel plants that surrounded half of Granite City were running close to capacity.

Traian paid $2,500 for their house. It had a fifteen-year mortgage, which required Traian to pay thirteen dollars per month. With Christina's frugal management of the household expenses, Traian was able to put twenty-five dollars of his monthly salary into a savings account. At that time, the stock market was growing at an unprecedented rate. Middle-class workers speculated in the stock market by buying stocks on margin with borrowed money. Traian resisted the temptation to participate in this easy money venture, which seemed too good to be true.

Although Traian was devoted to his family and generously gave of his spare time to see that their needs were met to the best of his ability, he did reserve a certain portion of his time for his own enjoyment. One example was his participation as a shortstop on the coke plant's baseball team.

Local baseball teams were common. They were not only made up of employees from several Granite City steel plants but also residents of adjacent small cities. During the summer months, Traian's team played every Sunday afternoon against one of the other teams in what was called the Trolley League. The name was adopted because most of the members from the visiting teams rode the streetcar in their uniforms to the home team's town on the day of the game. Traian thoroughly enjoyed his time on the ball field. It reminded him of his playing baseball in high school.

Christina put up with Traian's self-indulgence, which she thought was childish. She looked forward to the end of the baseball season.

Shortly after Jane's birth, Traian decided to make some major improvements to his house. This involved the construction of a new room on the back of the house, which would serve as a new kitchen. The existing kitchen would be converted into a dining room. In the bathroom, he decided to install a new bathtub, which was the fulfillment of a long overdue promise that he had made to Christina when they had first moved in.

Traian engaged a local contractor for the erection of the kitchen's shell. After the shell was built, he sought the help of his brother-in-law, Pete, who, with Traian's help, completed the interior. Pete built a workbench in the basement and attached a metal wood vise, which had been given to Traian by Ioan. Ioan had obtained it from one of his Romanian friends who had been a blacksmith. According to Ioan, the blacksmith had made the vise while he had been an apprentice. It had been part of the requirements for his admittance to the profession as a journeyman.

Traian's two boys, Billy and Johnny, looked forward to the weekends when Uncle Pete would come. They watched with interest and fascination as Uncle Pete threaded the ends of the galvanized water pipes, made electrical wire connections to light switches, nailed up drywall, and hung doors.

While all this was going on, Traian acted as his helper, handing him tools and assisting with the heavy lifting. When Christina asked Traian how the work was progressing, he replied, "Great! Pete is doing all the work that requires a skilled craftsman while I am doing the idiot work."

Christina laughed and teased him about only having *book learning* but no *common sense*. "I guess we determined that when we were dating," Traian rejoined with a smile. "Maybe when we get finished, Pete will give me a certificate that will identify me as the world's worst carpenter."

In a few months, the kitchen addition was complete, along with the new bathtub in the bathroom. Christina appreciated the extra room that the dining room allowed for her sewing and making of *palacinta* (a favorite Romanian pastry made with filo dough, which needs to be stretched over a floured tablecloth on the dining room table until it is paper-thin). The large blue enameled cooking range was moved into the new kitchen. This allowed room for the old couch-bed to be moved into the dining room.

Christina liked her old range, which had four gas burners on the right side and a sixteen-inch-wide coal-fired cooktop on the left. Two small gas ovens were above, and a large gas oven was below. Christina had the opportunity to bake bread and pies and cook a roast all at the same time. She also liked the coal-fired cooktop, particularly in winter, when it added additional heat to the kitchen while making a kettle of hot water available at all times.

When Traian asked her if she would like to have a new, more compact, modern-looking stove, she said, "Why should we waste money on a new stove when this one is still working fine? It just doesn't make good sense." The remark, which was made with a slightly demeaning inflection in her voice, took Traian by surprise. He was expecting a reply that was full of joy and thanks and not one that caused him to feel insulted.

Shortly after Billy was born, Traian decided to buy a car. If Teeny learned to drive, she could help by taking him to and from his job at the coke plant, even though it was only a mile away. This would give him an extra hour each day to be with his family. It would also provide an opportunity for Teeny to drive to downtown Granite City once in a while for shopping. The car could also be used for weekend drives to visit Christina's sister Anna and Traian's cousin Nick.

Because of Christina's constant concern about not spending money foolishly (such as for a new stove), Traian began to implement his strategic plan to acquire a family car. After about two weeks of brief, carefully spaced comments about the benefits of the car, with an emphasis on streetcar fares being saved and Sunday picnics taking place in Forest Park, he dropped the verbal tactic and began phase two.

Each evening after reading the *Star-Times* newspaper, which was delivered daily, he would remove the used-car page of the classified section and place it on top of the paper. He was hoping that Christina would notice it when she took the discarded newspaper to the basement where it would be saved for making fires in the furnace. A week later, he was very proud of himself when Christina said to him at the dinner table, "I think we should get a car."

Their first family car was a used Overland, which was a two-year-old, four-door sedan that was painted dark olive green. Traian, who already knew how to drive, took the family out to country roads on weekends where he would teach Christina to drive. She mastered control of the car and in a short time, passed the driver's test.

Their daily routine then changed. Instead of Traian starting his walk to work at 6:00 a.m., he left for work in the Overland next to Christina at 6:45 a.m. with their three children in the back seat still wearing their pajamas.

At 3:30 p.m., Christina would be waiting in the coke plant's parking lot, behind the wheel of the Overland, with the three children in the back seat. This time they would be dressed and cleaned up while anxiously looking for their father to come out with a smile on his face.

After supper, Traian read the newspaper while Christina did the dishes and the children played. At 8:00 p.m., the children, who were in their pajamas, and Traian spent a half hour in horseplay on the living room rug. Traian, who was on his hands and knees, was the horse. Johnny and Billy rode on his back urging him to move faster.

After several laps around the room, Traian would roll over while the two boys began to wrestle him. Traian lay on his back and tickled them while they tried to pin him to the floor. When Christina thought it was time for bed, she came in and put a stop to their roughhousing. They went into their bedroom giggling as they followed Traian, who was leading the way by walking on his hands.

The five years between 1924 and 1929 were good ones for Traian. He had a steady job, adequate wages, a comfortable life, and a growing savings account. The future looked bright.

Boat excursions on the Mississippi River were favorite pastimes for Traian and his family during the summer. In 1930, there were two excursion boats docked at the St. Louis Eads Bridge: the *JS* and the *Saint Paul*. The two wooden-hulled excursion boats were converted packet boats that had been built in 1896 in Dubuque, Iowa. At that time, the *JS* was named the *Quincy*. In 1919, there was no longer a need for passengers to travel on packet boats because they were using trains. The *Quincy* was converted into an excursion boat and named the *JS* to honor Captain John Streckfus, the owner.

For many years, the *JS* and its sister the *Saint Paul* held daytime excursions and evening moonlight cruises in St. Louis, which began on Memorial Day. Nothing was spared to make the new *JS* the most luxurious steamboat of the day.

The staterooms were removed from the second and third decks, opening the areas up for a dance floor and a posh dining/lounge area for the more affluent passengers. The second deck had wicker furniture with brightly colored cushions for the loungers and heavy tables with white linens for the diners, who were served by waiters in white jackets and black trousers. At the forward end of the deck, there was a half dome with ribs, which were supported by eight classic, iconic columns radiating from it. In the center of the half dome was a large Tiffany-glazed chandelier.

The first deck, which was formerly used as a cargo deck by the packet boat, was set aside for the less affluent passengers, who brought picnic baskets of food and jugs of lemonade. They placed these on tables located between the enclosed side wheels. Two large bright-red arms were hinged together. They converted the horizontal strokes of the piston rods to circular motions, which turned the side paddle wheels. This fascinated the children.

Early in the summer of 1931, Traian and Christina took Billy and Johnny on their first *JS* excursion. Jane, who was just one year old at that time, was being cared for by Ioan and Nanna Liana who had come to Traian's house for the weekend.

After parking his 1929 Chevrolet on the steep riverbank that was paved with granite stones, Traian led his family to the floating ticket house. He carried the picnic basket and a one-gallon jug of lemonade in while Christina followed, holding Johnny's hand.

At the ticket counter, Traian set down the food that he had been carrying and gave the ticket agent one and a half dollars, which covered the cost of the tickets for two adults and two children. After leaving the ticket house, they crossed a second gangway, which was over the water that separated the ticket house from the excursion boat. A crewman took the four tickets, which Traian held between the thumb and forefinger of the hand that was holding the jug, as they boarded.

Having been on *JS* excursions before, Traian knew precisely where to go. He quickly led his family past the refreshment stand, which was amidships, to the rows of tables and chairs near the stern between the two side wheels with the exposed driving arms.

It was an hour before departure, and choice table locations were still available near the rail just behind one of the side wheels. After staking out the family's territory by placing their picnic basket and jug at the end of one of the tables, Traian said, "We should go up to the top deck right away so we can get a good spot and see the boat shove off."

Christina grabbed the children's hands and followed Traian, leaving the picnic basket and jug unguarded. There seemed to have been an unwritten but understood code of trust among the less affluent passengers to respect the table territories and unguarded food that was left by passengers who were not at their claimed locations.

On the way to the stairs leading to the top deck, they passed the refreshment stand again. This time, they passed at a slower pace, allowing Billy to see a large glass cylinder that was full of a bright-green soft drink.

"What is that green stuff behind the counter?" he asked Traian as he held his father back for an answer.

"It's called a Green River," Traian replied without stopping. He knew that Billy wanted a glass and gave him a reply before the question was asked. "You don't need any of that. We have plenty of lemonade." Traian was practicing the advice that had been given to him by Ioan while Traian was growing up.

"Watch the pennies, and the dollars will take care of themselves," Ioan would often say. "If you always buy yourself little things that you don't need each time you want them, you will never have money for the big things when you need them," was another one of Ioan's pearls of wisdom.

When they arrived at the top deck, Traian took his family to the dock's side of the deck, where they found four empty deck chairs. They reclined in them as they waited for the boat to leave its docked position. A sudden burst of the steam calliope startled Billy as it began puffing Steven Foster melodies. Traian took the boys to the calliope, which was located behind the pilothouse, so that they could see the man depressing the keys of the huge steam instrument. Christina remained seated in her deck chair and saved the other three chairs for their return.

At 10:00 a.m., the calliope stopped playing, and the steamboat's whistle gave two long blasts from the pilothouse, signaling the boat's departure. Upon reaching the pilothouse on their way back to Christina, Traian raised up each child so that he could see the pilot and return his wave. When they got back to Christina, Traian went immediately to the rail and watched the dockworkers remove the thick ropes from their mooring masts. It reminded him of his departure on the *Carpathia* twenty-two years earlier.

On their way back to the first deck, Traian stopped his family at the stairs that led to the second deck, where the more affluent passengers were being served food and drinks, playing bridge, and reclining in colorful wicker lounge chairs. His thoughts again took him to the *Carpathia*. He remembered when he had gone to the first-class-passenger area for a look at how wealthy people lived.

A frown from one of the *JS* waiters in a white jacket reminded him that he did not belong in that part of the boat. He immediately ushered his family back to where they belonged. He resolved that someday, he would ride in first class on a boat if he watched his pennies and didn't waste his money on little things that they wanted but didn't need.

The Half Dome on the *J.S.*

The *J.S.* at the Eads Bridge

CHAPTER 9
THE GREAT DEPRESSION

The prosperity of the Roaring Twenties began to end in 1929 with the crash of the stock market. The middle-class investors who had profited by buying stocks on margin with borrowed money suddenly found themselves deeply in debt. Those like Traian who had a savings account were faced with the possibility of losing their life's savings because banks threatened to fail as people made withdrawals from their savings accounts.

Traian was thankful that he had not gambled and bought stocks on margin. He had a little over $1,500 in his savings account. He owed a little less than $1,400 on his mortgage before he could pay off the loan that he had received for the down payment on his house. He also was able to save $25 each month after paying the $13-per-month mortgage payment.

Because of the uncertainty of whether his employment would continue, Traian decided to save as much money as he could while he still had a job. Layoffs from the steel companies surrounding Granite City were high. Granite City was among one of the hardest hit in the United States at the beginning of the Great Depression.

Traian determined that if he wanted to continue his present standard of living, it would be in his best interest to use the money in his savings account to pay off his mortgage before a run was made on the bank. Since the bank where he had his savings account also held his mortgage, Traian thought this would not present a problem, but he was wrong. At first, the bank refused to make the transaction. Traian had to hire an attorney to act on his behalf before he was able to pay off the mortgage.

Rather than leaving any money in his savings account, he decided to rent a safe-deposit box. For the past five years, he had been paying ten dollars a month to his father. On his present wages minus the ten dollars, he would be able to save fifty dollars a month. He began buying small government bonds as cash began to accumulate in his safe-deposit box. Because of his difficult experience when trying to pay off his mortgage, Traian had lost confidence in banks.

The Great Depression had little adverse effect on Ioan. After several years of working in the painting department of the Ford Motor Company, Ioan began working for a painting contractor. More than half the houses that were built at that time had wood siding, which needed to be painted once every four or five years for proper maintenance. Because Ioan could cover a large area with paint in a short amount of time, he earned a good reputation among painting contractors who competed for his services.

Ioan was always busy. With the rent from the upstairs apartment, along with a steady income from painting, Ioan was able to pay off the mortgage on his house at Dresden and Eichelberger by 1928.

There was a woman in the St. Louis Romanian community who lost her husband shortly before Johanna had died. Nanna Liana reminded Ioan of Johanna. They began seeing each other regularly at Sunday church services and other Romanian functions. Nanna Liana had a son, John, who also was about Traian's age. Out of a combination of mutual attraction and loneliness, they began seeing more and more of each other and were soon married.

Nanna Liana's son, John, and Traian, who both approved of the union, began a brotherly relationship and visited each other occasionally. John and his wife, Doasha, lived on a small farm in St. Louis County.

On one of Traian and Christina's visits, Traian and John were about to leave to go rabbit hunting when Christina said, "Now don't forget the salt."

Billy, who was four years old, asked, "Why do you need salt?"

Christina answered while smiling at Traian, "All good hunters sprinkle salt on the rabbit's tail before they shoot it," she said while Billy still had a look of confusion on his face.

After several hours, the two hunters came back empty-handed. "Why no rabbits?" asked Christina.

"We ran out of salt," Traian replied, smiling. Billy was still confused. Later, his father told him that it was an old Romanian joke. "Billy, if you get close enough to a rabbit to put salt on its tail, you don't need a gun," said Traian. Billy finally understood but did not think it was funny.

In 1930, Ioan began to consider returning to Romania. As he did in 1907 when he was contemplating a move to America, he began to examine costs and benefits. With the money that he had saved and the value of the house on Dresden and Eichelberger, he calculated that he would be able to pay for first-class passage tickets to Europe, buy a small farm in Beba Veche, and live comfortably for the rest of his life.

Ever since he had come to America, he had been maintaining regular correspondence with his cousin Simion, who had given him firsthand knowledge of property prices and the cost of living in Romania. Many small farms had been made available when large landowners had broken up their properties after the end of World War I in the province of Banat. Before World War I, Banat had been ruled by Austria-Hungary. Because over 80 percent of Banat's inhabitants were Romanian peasants, it became part of the Romanian government after the war.

Simion had been keeping Ioan abreast of small farms' prices in his recent letters. Ioan was convinced that his numbers were realistic. The whole idea made sense to him. Survival had always been his first priority. With his children now being self-sufficient, he no longer saw himself as the provider of his family.

Instead, he saw himself as a future burden to them in his old age. He thought that his enjoyment of visiting his children and grandchildren, at this time in his life, was a selfish desire. He thought about the sacrifices of caring for him in his old age.

At the same time, he had a desire to see the old country again and to reestablish his deep feelings for his Romanian heritage. Whether the decision to return to Romania was an act of selfishness or generosity, Ioan felt that he had earned and deserved the right to make the decision to return.

Not being able to see his grandchildren grow up was a sacrifice that Ioan found difficult to make. He made a point of seeing them as much as possible by offering to babysit so that Traian and Christina could enjoy afternoons out together.

On one such occasion, Billy asked, "Grandpa, can I go out to play?"

"Yes," Ioan answered. "You can play in the backyard but stay out of the alley."

A half hour later, Ioan decided to check on Billy by looking out the kitchen window. Billy was nowhere to be seen. *I'll bet he's playing in the alley behind the garage*, Ioan thought as he briskly walked through the backyard. His assumption was correct. He found Billy rummaging in a basket of tin cans and broken glass behind the garage.

"Didn't I tell you not to go out into the alley?" Ioan said in an angry voice as he grabbed Billy's arm and swatted him several times across his rear. Billy immediately burst into tears and continued to cry as Ioan led him back into the house.

When they got inside, Ioan took out his handkerchief and dried Billy's eyes while saying to him in a kind and loving voice, "The reason I told you not to go into the alley was because I was afraid you would hurt yourself with all that broken glass."

On another occasion, he saw Billy scribbling on the chalkboard that Santa Claus had left him on the previous Christmas. It was a twenty-four-by-eighteen-inch blackboard that bridged two A-frames, which were hinged at the top. Across the bottom, there was a tray for chalk and an eraser.

Ioan walked up to the blackboard, grabbed the eraser, and removed Billy's scribbling while saying, "Let's pretend we are in school and Grandpa's your teacher." Billy, who was only four years old at the time, did not answer but looked with interest as Ioan wrote the numbers one through nine across the top of the board.

Then handing the chalk to Billy, Ioan said, "Now you write the same numbers under the ones Grandpa wrote, and I will tell you their names as you write them." Billy, with some effort, started to draw the numbers as Grandpa recited their names. When he got to number eight, Billy hesitated. He slowly made a circle and then turned toward Ioan with a questioning look.

"That's fine," Ioan said. "Now just make a bigger one downstairs." Billy finished his number eight and then immediately proceeded to write a number nine with another small circle followed by a vertical stroke on the right side.

"Good work, Billy," Ioan said as he picked him up and kissed him on the cheek. Billy cringed during the kiss. He didn't like the feeling of Ioan's mustache brushing across his face.

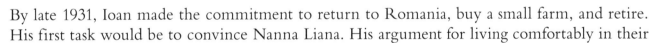

By late 1931, Ioan made the commitment to return to Romania, buy a small farm, and retire. His first task would be to convince Nanna Liana. His argument for living comfortably in their old age convinced her.

Together, they went to their children to tell them their plans. Ioan was firm in his decision, even though the comments from his children about the enjoyment he gave them with his physical presence softened his heart. He did not change his decision. He booked passage on the *Mauretania* for their return to the old country.

This time, they traveled first class. When he arrived at Beba Veche, he found the property he was looking for. He immediately sent a picture of himself and Nanna Liana standing in front of the house to Traian.

By 1934, the Great Depression hit hard in Granite City. Because the Depression was worldwide, overseas shipments of steel from Granite City declined sharply and large layoffs took place. Pete, Christina's brother, was included.

Without a regular income, Pete made up for it by utilizing his manual and entrepreneurial skills to obtain small amounts of money from a variety of sources. He made trellises out of lattice strips, painted them white, and sold them throughout the neighborhood. They consisted of several different geometric designs, which demonstrated not only his manual skills but also his creative imagination. He also became an insurance agent and a real estate agent. The barbershop, which he had set up on the front porch of his house on Hodges Avenue, became a marketing opportunity for the trellises and his insurance sales.

Pete had an engaging personality. He always smiled and was pleasant and genuinely interested in other people.

One example of this was his friendship with a young neighbor named Paul Hawk. Paul, who was of Native American descent, was gifted with a great singing voice. Amateur contests featuring entertainers who were looking for recognition were very popular at that time. The contestant who received the loudest applause was the winner of the contest. Pete encouraged Paul to enter these contests and recruited friends and neighbors to meet at the barbershop on the day of the contest. They loaded the few cars that were available with people and went to the contest, where they clapped and yelled as loud as they could after Paul's performance.

In 1932, Traian learned from the *St. Louis Star-Times* that in 1933, there would be a world's fair in Chicago. Traian thought it would be nice to take his family to Chicago for about a week to visit the fair. He accomplished his first step by arranging with his superiors at the coke plant to have his vacation the first two weeks in June. He then began correspondence with his aunt Vasilka, who lived in Chicago. It was Traian's plan for the family to spend a week in Chicago with his aunt and her husband.

It was common in those days for Romanian families to visit each other for a week at a time. Sleeping arrangements were made available with living room couches and pallets on the floor with blankets and pillows. It was Traian's strategy that if he regularly corresponded with Aunt Vasilka and mentioned his interest in coming to the Chicago World's Fair, she would invite the family to spend a week with her and her husband.

To persuade Christina, he used the same tactic as he had used with buying their first car. He made sure that every article that he could find in the newspaper or any other printed material about the coming fair was placed in a conspicuous location for Christina to see and hopefully read.

The strategy worked. Early in 1933, a letter from Aunt Vasilka arrived, inviting Traian and his family to be their guests in Chicago and to see the Chicago World's Fair, which had been named the Century of Progress. By this time, Christina was showing great interest in seeing the fair after reading the articles Traian had provided.

The three-hundred-mile trip to Chicago in the 1929 gray two-door Chevy began at noon. They arrived at their destination at 9:00 p.m. Aunt Vasilka and her husband lived on the first level of a three-story apartment building. Sleeping accommodations were made: Traian and Christina would sleep in the spare bedroom, and their three children would sleep on pallets in the living room. Afterward, Aunt Vasilka fed her five guests the stew that she had prepared. She had anticipated that they would arrive hungry. She was right. Her guests, who were tired and hungry from the trip, ate their fill before bedding down for the night.

Early the next morning and after eating a breakfast prepared by Aunt Vasilka, the family was on their way to the fair, which was located in an area south of the Field Museum along the shore of Lake Michigan. As they walked from the parking lot to the main entrance, they were able to see the signature feature of the fair: the sky ride, which consisted of two large towers spaced about 1,850 feet apart. The towers, which were over 600 feet tall, enclosed elevators. The elevators took observers to the 200-foot level, where they boarded suspended cable cars. The cars traveled from one tower to the other, giving passengers a spectacular view of the entire fairgrounds and Lake Michigan.

Traian and Christina had planned to devote their first day at the fair to their children. One section of the fair was called Enchanted Island, which was set aside entirely for the interests of children. It was an amusement park with rides, haunted houses, curved mirrors, and clowns. Traian and Christina took advantage of this time to rest from the previous day's long ride while watching their children giggle and scream during their day at Enchanted Island.

The next day, Traian and Christina went to the fair by themselves while Aunt Vasilka, accompanied by her sister, Aunt Savitia, took the children to Lincoln Park for the day. Traian and Christina entered the fair from the Sixteenth Street entrance. It was about a three-block walk from the parking lot, which took them across the pedestrian bridge over the Illinois Central Railroad tracks.

"Let's go on the sky ride first, Teeny. That way we will be able to see the whole fair from above."

Christina had reservations. To begin with, she was afraid of heights. She was also uncertain about the safety of the large cable cars that were suspended on what seemed to be very thin wires. Nevertheless, she knew that Traian wanted to take the ride very much. "Okay," she said reluctantly. She thought that if she kept her eyes closed during the ride, she would be able to handle it.

It was a short walk from the Sixteenth Street entrance to the west tower. After paying eighty cents for two tickets, they entered the elevator. It took them up 220 feet to the platform where they boarded the cable car, which held thirty-six passengers. It was a terrifying four-minute ride for Christina. Even with her eyes closed, she felt the car's vertical movement, which came from the stretching cables above, and the horizontal movement, which came from the force of the wind.

Traian, on the other hand, thoroughly enjoyed the trip. He viewed the lagoon below, the entire fair to the left and to the right, and Lake Michigan straight ahead.

Christina was thankful when the car finally arrived at the east tower. For her, the four-minute trip had seemed like a half hour. To Traian, it had been the shortest four minutes of his life. It wasn't until the elevator door opened at ground level that her heart rate went back to normal.

"Let's go visit the House of Tomorrow," Christina said to Traian.

Traian looked for it on the map. It was about a mile south of the east tower. "It will be a very long walk, Teeny," Traian responded.

"I don't care how far it is. You had your sky ride. Now it's my turn," Teeny said.

The long walk took them past the Streets of Paris, where Christina hastened their walking pace. Then they passed the Hawaiian Village, the Hungarian Pavilion, the Italian Village, the Spanish Village, the Irish Village, and the English Village before they got to the home section. It consisted of eight houses in a row, with the House of Tomorrow at the far south end.

There they witnessed, with amazement, the residential under-the-counter dishwasher, a washing machine that spun-dried clothes, a clothes dryer, and a steam iron. Most interesting of all was the television research. Christina imagined herself living in a house where she would not need to run washed clothes through a wringer, hang them on a clothesline, or dampen them before ironing. She also found it hard to believe that they now made radios that allowed you to see people who were miles away talking and moving.

"Do you think we will ever live to see all this in the average home?" she asked Traian.

"I think we will, if we live long enough," Traian responded.

Late in 1933, the coke plant shut down and Traian lost his job. He had been anticipating this for some time. While visiting Aunt Vasilka in Chicago, he had noticed in the newspaper's classified section that there were a number of job openings, which had surprised him. With no opportunities immediately available in Granite City and little hope for the future, Traian decided to go to Chicago, stay with Aunt Vasilka, and look for a job that would fit his abilities and the needs of his family.

Once he was established with a permanent job and a place to stay, he would bring his family. As he was making these plans, he thought about the similarity to the situation his father had faced when he had left Romania.

Shortly after arriving in Chicago, he got a job at a coke plant and began looking for a place to live. In the meantime, Christina kept reading the help-wanted ads, hoping to find an opportunity for Traian to return. She did not like moving away from Pete and Anna and having to make new friends in Chicago. However, she accepted the fact that steady work for Traian was their first priority.

Her prayers were answered when she learned that Shell Oil Company in Roxanna, a small town five miles from Granite City, was expanding and was hiring new employees. Traian was contacted, and he returned to Granite City.

Traian's first job at the Shell Oil Company was that of a gauger. Huge storage tanks surrounded the distilleries. Some had crude oil, which was awaiting refinement in a still. Others had gasoline, which was awaiting shipment to customers. In the spring and the fall, the air above the product that was stored in the enclosed tanks condensed on the inside of the tanks and resulted in water settling at the bottom of the tank. The oil was below while the lighter product was above. It was the gauger's job to drop a long wooden pole through a port in the top of the tank to the bottom. The pole, which was marked off in feet and inches, was lowered to the bottom of the tank and then withdrawn. The gauger read and recorded the product level in the tank as indicated by the oil-moistened surface on the pole.

It bothered Traian that the reading on the pole's gauge did not reflect the amount of water in the bottom of the tank. To get an accurate reading, the water level in the bottom of the tank should be determined and subtracted from the reading of the product level. On his own and with his knowledge of chemistry, Traian set up a small laboratory in his basement and produced a salve that could be placed on the bottom fourteen inches of the pole. The salve had a chemical that would show a different color when the water level was reached. Traian demonstrated this product to his boss. He was soon promoted to the operation of one of the stills.

In 1934, government programs were in place to assist the large number of unemployed people. Relief stations were set up where the unemployed could come weekly and obtain food. At those locations, those needing medical attention could obtain a voucher that would assure government payment to physicians for an office visit. Churches held weekly card parties to pay off mortgages on construction projects, which had been started in the Roaring Twenties.

Although his wage at Shell Oil Company was adequate for their standard of living and budgeted savings, the adverse effects of the Great Depression on many families in Granite City gave them concern about the security of Traian's present employment. During their discussions on ways to get extra income on a regular basis, the possibility of setting up a beauty shop in their home came up.

"I like the idea, John, but I don't know if I would be admitted to a beauty school with only a grade-school education."

"I really think you could do it, Teeny," Traian replied with encouragement. "You're a lot smarter than you think you are."

Christina soon found herself enrolled in the Maranella Beauty School in St. Louis. Traian, knowing the importance a quality education, had done some research on the schools that had been available. The Maranella School had received the reputation of being the most difficult. This had led Traian to believe that it was probably the best in the area.

It was a six-month course. Christina got up early each morning and took the streetcar to downtown St. Louis after preparing breakfast for her three children. Traian took Jane to Pete and Irene's house on his way to work while Johnny and Billy walked to Sacred Heart School for the 8:00 a.m. mass, which took place before school started.

On his way home from work, Traian picked up Jane from Pete's house and then started preparing supper while awaiting Christina's return from beauty school. After supper, Christina studied while Traian did the dishes and the children played. At 8:00 p.m., the children were in bed, and Traian sat next to Christina at the dining room table. She was studying subjects related to muscles, nerves, and blood circulation. She needed to know these subjects for her final exam at Maranella, as well as for the state examinations she would need to take before she could open her shop at home. During this time, Traian acted as Christina's tutor, explaining the meaning of words she did not understand and clarifying complex concepts with simplified analogies in words that Christina understood.

After six months, Christina passed her finals at Maranella and the Illinois and Missouri state examinations with very high marks. These accomplishments increased her self-confidence and self-esteem. Traian was also proud of her while sensing that the book-learning gap between them was beginning to close.

It was now time to set up the beauty shop. Once again, Traian called upon Pete to help. A small bedroom was partitioned off in the basement for Billy and Johnny. The front bedroom was converted into the shop. On the partition that separated the bedroom from the bathroom, Pete installed a lavatory, which was a portable drain board with a piece cut out for the necks of customers who were being shampooed. Along the partition separating the bedroom from the living room, there was a small kitchen table and a wall mirror where Christina would be able to cut hair, set hair, and place hair in rollers for permanents.

At that time, permanents were made by electric permanent-wave machines, which clamped over hair that was covered in a solution and placed in rollers. They heated the hair a given amount of time, which was determined by the beautician based on the fineness and texture of the hair. The hair clamps were connected by wires to the machine. The machine was supported by a pole on casters, which allowed the machine to be moved about when necessary.

The front porch was enclosed in glass and converted to a drying area, where two dryers were set up. Since personal appearance was part of a woman's self-esteem and vanity, Traian thought the word *vanity* should be a part of the shop's name. Christina liked the idea but also wanted it known that she was a graduate of a highly recognized beauty school. Together, they composed the thirty-by-forty-eight- inch metal sign that was placed under the eaves of the front porch. The sign was set perpendicular to the front of the house so that it could be read at a distance by anyone coming from any direction. The sign read:

VANITY FAIR BEAUTY SHOP
(Maranella Graduate)

With the opening of the beauty shop, it was necessary to have a telephone installed so that people could call for appointments. Several hours after the phone had been installed, Traian told Christina that he needed to go to the store for a few things and left. Shortly after he left, the phone rang, and Christina answered it.

"Hello," Christina said.

"Is this the Vanity Fair Beauty Shop?" asked the male voice on the other end of the line.

"Yes," replied Christina.

"Do you work on both males and females?"

Christina was puzzled and answered with some hesitation. "Uh, yes, I guess. What do you need?"

"Well, I have a dirty old shaggy male dog that badly needs a shampoo."

"Oh, John," Christina said with a laugh. "When you come home, I am going to box your ears."

In a short time, the sign brought in customers. Christina's skills as a beautician resulted in referrals. She soon found herself busy most of the day. Traian, knowing that she was tired after being on her feet all day, began pitching in by helping with the cooking and washing. Christina thoroughly enjoyed her new role in assisting with the income as well as being a mother. She loved talking with her customers during the day. It took some time before she agreed with Traian that they should have someone clean the house periodically to give them both a little relief. In a short time, the income from the shop paid off the start-up expenses, and their savings began to grow again. This allowed them to purchase more government bonds.

However, Traian was still looking for a safety net in case he was laid off from Shell Oil Company. He began to go to night school at Rankin Trade School and studied air-conditioning and refrigeration. In spite of the shortage of money, Traian saw that more and more retail stores were beginning to cool their establishments with air-conditioning systems to get a leg up on their competitors. Traian learned how to compute cooling requirements and to size equipment for systems so that he would have some kind of backup skill to offer in case he was laid off.

It was not, however, all work and no play for Traian and Christina. They both enjoyed the same kinds of recreation and entertainment.

Sundays were set aside for the family's enjoyment. In the summer, they went to Forest Park, the site of the 1904 World's Fair, where they spent time at the zoo and the art museum. The family also went swimming together. Most of the time, Traian took them to locations where swimming was free like the Meramec River near St. Louis or the Gabret Slough in Granite City, where the water was less muddy and the bottom was sandy. In the winter, there was ice skating at Long Lake near Granite City or sledding down Art Hill in front of the art museum in Forest Park.

For the most part, Traian looked for free recreation. On occasion, he did indulge in the cost of certain events such as a baseball game at Sportsman's Park to see the St. Louis Cardinals' Gas House Gang play. On those days, Traian, Billy, and Johnny went while Christina and Jane stayed home.

In the summer, the family looked forward to going on a trip to the St. Louis Municipal Opera. Early in the evening of the performance, they took advantage of the free seats. They attended circuses and carnivals when they came to St. Louis and Granite City. Special events like the Ice Capades and other similar events that Traian particularly wanted to see filled evenings with entertainment for the family.

Along with the family recreation and entertainment outings, there were events that tightened the ties on family relationships. During the summer, Anna's children, Nickey and Helen, would spend a week playing with Johnny, Billy, and Jane in Granite City. Billy and Johnny would also spend a week with Nickey and Helen in St. Louis at their home on Dresden and Eichelberger. They all played together in Christy Park. They went fishing in the ponds at Carondelet Park, which was about a mile away.

Helen, who was about four years older than Johnny, was just starting high school. She provided a little culture and knowledge to the younger ones. She taught them how to play chess and to identify constellations in the night sky. She took them on the bus to the St. Louis Municipal Opera where she also took advantage of the free seats.

Traian wanted the family to retain its Romanian heritage. Several times a year, he took the family to the Romanian Orthodox church at 1427 Missouri Avenue, in the Soulard area, just across from Lafayette Park.

The church was founded in 1935 by Bucur, the godfather of Johnny and Billy. Bucur, who was Traian's age, had three children: Billy, Tommy, and Marie. They were all near the ages of Traian's children. Traian and Bucur, although not blood related, maintained a close social relationship. Traian and his family usually visited Bucur and his family on Sundays at Bucur's residence, which was above his tavern and restaurant on Kingshighway near Vandeventer. Just as his father had, Bucur called his business The Place. Traian looked upon Bucur as a well-respected leader of the Romanian community in St. Louis, from whom many Romanians often sought advice.

In the spring of 1936, Traian was called to the office of his supervisor. Sitting in the office of the supervisor and dressed in a business suit was a man Traian had not seen before.

"Johnny, meet Alex," said the supervisor. "Alex is a Shell employee from Romania who has come to Roxana to lead the design and construction of a new still. You have been selected to be his assistant. You will acquaint him with the refinery, answer his questions, and help him in any way you can. Don't worry. He speaks English just as good as you and me."

Alex rose from his chair and shook Traian's hand. "Hello, Johnny, I am looking forward to working with you."

With the smile of a jester, Traian replied in Romanian, "Good day. The pleasure will be mine. From what city in Romania did you come?" Both Alex and the supervisor were surprised that Traian spoke fluent Romanian. The supervisor sat at his desk, stunned, while Alex and Traian exchanged pleasantries with a few more comments to each other in Romanian.

Out of courtesy, Alex cut off the conversation in Romanian and said to the supervisor, "This is great. You have been able to find me an assistant who speaks Romanian." The supervisor, who was still stunned by the coincidence, did not reply.

Alex, a highly respected engineer of Shell Oil Company, was able to bring his wife and three-year-old daughter to the United States while he was on his special assignment. As an additional perk, he was provided with a car.

Traian and Alex got along very well as the design and construction of the new still progressed. With his knowledge of chemistry and hands-on experience of the oil-distilling process, Traian became acquainted with the design criteria and the thought process that Alex had put into his plans for the new still.

While the still was under construction, the families of Traian and Alex developed a close social relationship. Alex's wife, who could drive, often came over during the day with her daughter and chatted with Christina between appointments. On weekends, Alex came with them, at which time, Traian was able to learn Alex's opinions and predictions about the political climate in Romania.

In 1936, Hitler's Nazi party was well established. There was a strong fascist movement in Romania, which was headed by Ion Antonescu. Ion was at odds with Nicolae Iorga. Iorga was still publishing his newspaper *Sămănătorul* (*The Sower*). Russia was looking into the possibility of annexing Bessarabia, the Romanian province that was along Russia's western border.

"Well, John," Alex said. "Romania has two choices: side with Hitler and become fascist or side with Russia and become communist and lose Bessarabia. Personally, I feel that becoming fascist would be better. Our way of life would not change as much as it would if we were communists. Either way, things don't look good for Romania."

TRAIAN'S SECOND HOME IN ST.LOUIS
AT DRESDEN AND EICHELBERGER

Bill, Jane & Johnny
Lincoln Park, Chicago 1933

Mauretania
The Ship That Took Ioan and Nana Liana Back To Romania

**Ioan & Nana Liana at their Retirement Home in Romania
1936**

**Ioan's Retirement Home in Romania
2004**

1933 Chicago World's Fair Skyride

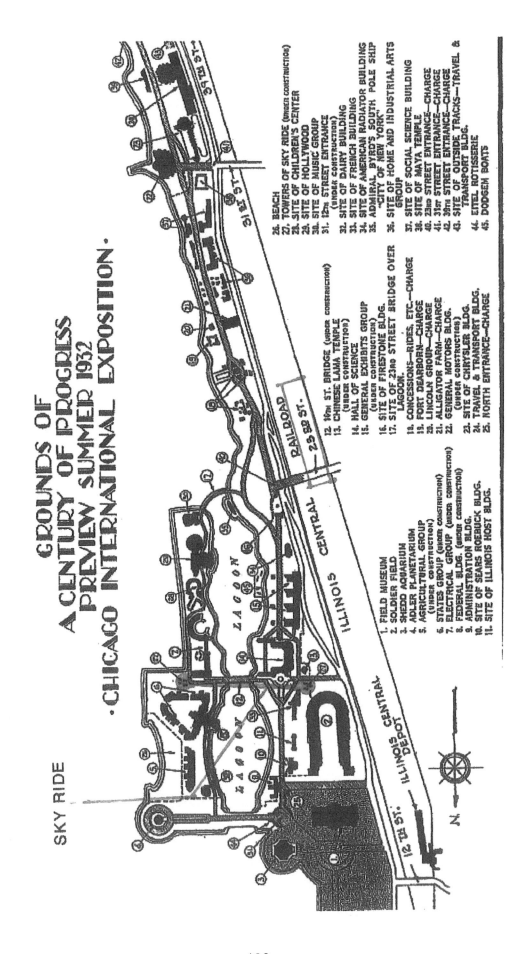

SKY RIDE

GROUNDS OF
A CENTURY OF PROGRESS
PREVIEW SUMMER 1932
·CHICAGO INTERNATIONAL EXPOSITION·

1. FIELD MUSEUM
2. SOLDIER FIELD
3. SHEDD AQUARIUM
4. ADLER PLANETARIUM
5. AGRICULTURAL GROUP (UNDER CONSTRUCTION)
6. STATES GROUP (UNDER CONSTRUCTION)
7. ELECTRICAL GROUP (UNDER CONSTRUCTION)
8. FEDERAL BLDG. (UNDER CONSTRUCTION)
9. ADMINISTRATION BLDG.
10. SITE OF SEARS ROEBUCK BLDG.
11. SITE OF ILLINOIS HOST BLDG.

12. 16th ST. BRIDGE (UNDER CONSTRUCTION)
13. CHINESE LAMA TEMPLE (UNDER CONSTRUCTION)
14. HALL OF SCIENCE
15. GENERAL EXHIBITS GROUP (UNDER CONSTRUCTION)
16. SITE OF FIRESTONE BLDG.
17. SITE OF 23rd STREET BRIDGE OVER LAGOON.
18. CONCESSIONS—RIDES, ETC.—CHARGE
19. FORT DEARBORN—CHARGE
20. LINCOLN GROUP—CHARGE
21. ALLIGATOR FARM—CHARGE
22. GENERAL MOTORS BLDG. (UNDER CONSTRUCTION)
23. SITE OF CHRYSLER BLDG.
24. TRAVEL & TRANSPORT BLDG.
25. NORTH ENTRANCE—CHARGE

26. BEACH
27. TOWERS OF SKY RIDE (UNDER CONSTRUCTION)
28. SITE OF CHILDREN'S CENTER
29. SITE OF HOLLYWOOD
30. SITE OF MUSIC GROUP
31. 12th STREET ENTRANCE (UNDER CONSTRUCTION)
32. SITE OF DAIRY BUILDING
33. SITE OF FRENCH BUILDING
34. SITE OF AMERICAN RADIATOR BUILDING
35. ADMIRAL BYRD'S SOUTH POLE SHIP "CITY OF NEW YORK"
36. SITE OF HOME AND INDUSTRIAL ARTS GROUP
37. SITE OF SOCIAL SCIENCE BUILDING
38. SITE OF MAYA TEMPLE
39. 23rd STREET ENTRANCE—CHARGE
40. 31st STREET ENTRANCE—CHARGE
42. 39th STREET ENTRANCE—CHARGE
43. SITE OF OUTSIDE TRACKS—TRAVEL & TRANSPORT BLDG.
44. EITEL ROTISSERIE
45. DODGEM BOATS

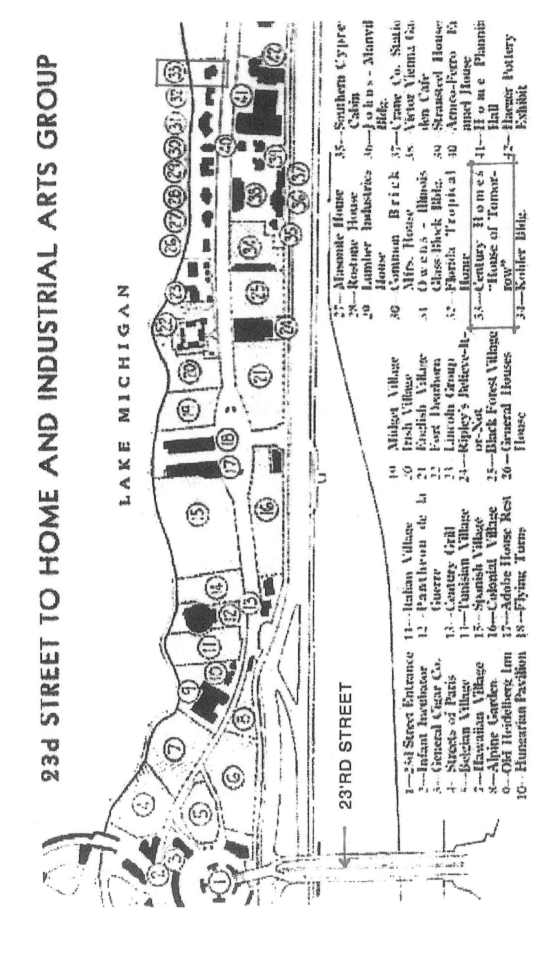

Entrance, Enchanted Island
A Century of Progress

THEATRE

1933 Chicago World's Fair
Entrance to the Enchanted Island, The Children's Fairyland

Skyride View To The North

CHAPTER 10
WORLD WAR II

With the frantic mobilization that came after Pearl Harbor, the coke plant in Granite City reopened, and Traian was offered a job as assistant superintendent of the coke ovens and by-products division, which he accepted with great enthusiasm. He was now on salary with a bonus at the end of the year, which was based on the productivity of his department.

This opportunity to increase his savings and to purchase more bonds caused him to wonder if he was doing the best thing. He sought Bucur's advice.

Bucur told him that he thought the value of industrial stocks would increase because of the war effort and that he should take advantage of it by balancing his savings with stocks as well as bonds. He also suggested that Traian engage a financial advisor to assist him with his stock purchases. He cautioned him to find someone who would not buy and sell stocks only for the commission. Traian took Bucur's advice and found a young financial advisor whom he could trust in Clayton, Missouri.

In the fall of 1942, Johnny was taken to Glenwood Sanitarium, a private psychiatric hospital in Webster Groves, Missouri. For the previous three months, his behavior had been gradually changing. He began acting strangely, complained of hearing voices, and became a discipline problem. Christina thought that he was just going through a difficult adolescent phase and that all he needed was a combination of good parental advice, counseling, and stronger discipline. Traian, on the other hand, saw things differently and suspected psychiatric problems. Traian made an appointment to speak with Dr. Reuss where he explained Johnny's behavior in detail.

"John, from what you told me, I think Johnny needs the help of a psychiatrist."

"Can you recommend one?" asked Traian.

"There is a Dr. Schwalb who heads up a private psychiatric hospital in Webster Groves," advised Dr. Reuss. "He would be my first choice. The only other option would be to have him committed to the state-run psychiatric hospital in Alton, which of course, would be a lot less expensive."

Traian cringed at the thought of Alton, which was referred to by the local residents as "The insane asylum," and was the subject of many jokes and weird stories. The stigma of having a mental disease was high at that time, due to the lack of public understanding.

After sharing the options given by Dr. Reuss with Christina, she agreed with Traian that Glenwood would be the best choice.

Dr. Schwalb's diagnosis was schizophrenia. The only treatments, at the time, were electric shock treatments, hydrotherapy, and psychoanalysis. Drug therapy was just beginning. The costs for hospitalization and Dr. Schwalb's fees seemed surprisingly high to Traian.

"How long will he need to be cared for?" Traian asked Dr. Schwalb.

"To be honest, I really can't tell you, but he will need to stay in the hospital for at least three months," Dr. Schwalb said.

During the three months, Traian and Christina visited Johnny regularly but saw no signs of improvement. Christina was struggling with what she may have done wrong to cause this to happen to Johnny and what she could do now to help him get better. Each day, she became more and more depressed with helplessness and frustration. Christina's concern about Johnny's condition had become so great that she agreed that she should be admitted to Glenwood for evaluation and treatment. She was feeling so miserable that she would do almost anything to get relief.

Traian was now faced with the sobering reality of caring for his entire family, with two in the hospital, one near the end of grade school, and one about halfway through high school. As medical expenses rose, he had no idea of when they would end or how much the total cost would be. He began to approach his problem with a certain grit and Romanian determination, which he had inherited from his father. He broke his problems into pieces and priorities and figured out what resources he had at hand.

His first concern was Jane, who was reaching puberty without a mother's guidance. "She needs the kind of parental guidance that only you can give her," Traian pleaded over the phone with Flora, who was living in Emporia, Kansas, with her husband and two young children. Because of Flora's pity for Traian and her deep sense of family unity, she was more than happy for Jane to come and live with her while Traian worked through his problems.

Next, he must decide how he would deal with the rising medical expenses. He was determined that Teeny and John would get the best medical care available, regardless of the cost. His uncertainty was what the cost would be. Traian decided to find a way to supplement his income by renting out the upper level of his house while he and Bill lived in the basement.

Pete was called on again. He removed the shampoo sink and installed a shower, toilet, and small gas range in the basement. With that arrangement, Traian and Bill would only use the rear entrance, which was located midway between the upstairs and basement. That way, they wouldn't interfere with the privacy of the renters.

At that time, there was an army engineers' depot, which had been recently established in Granite City along the Mississippi River, where military equipment was received, stored, and distributed by barges. Many soldiers and their wives were stationed at the depot and were looking for places to live. Traian found two nice couples to rent the upstairs. He was then able to count on some extra money to offset his growing medical expenses.

Near the end of 1943, Traian was disappointed with the lack of progress in Christina's and Johnny's conditions. After further investigation of the conditions and care that was available at Alton, he determined the same level of care was being given at Alton as it was at Glenwood. He decided to send one of them to Alton. The question was, which one should he send?

When he discussed the issue with Dr. Schwalb, he was advised that Christina had a better chance of overcoming her depression than Johnny had of being cured of schizophrenia. Christina was transferred to Alton after being examined by the admitting team of doctors. In a month, her condition improved dramatically, and a hearing was set for her dismissal. Traian was happy with Christina's progress and looked forward to her coming home, but Christina had other ideas.

While recovering from her depression in Alton, she began questioning her relationship with Traian. The memories of her rushed-into marriage with Traian, which had been deep in her subconscious, suddenly came forward. She needed some time to live independently to sort out her feelings. Traian, grateful that Teeny was no longer consumed with depression, assisted Christina with loving empathy. He thought that the independence that she so badly needed would be temporary.

I won her love once, and I can do it again, he thought while he helped her locate an apartment in St. Louis near the beauty shop where Christina found employment. Traian gave Christina as much space as he could. He only visited her occasionally to make sure that her physical needs were being met. He was careful not to appear to be putting any pressure on her to make her change her mind.

While Christina sorted out her feelings, Traian actively made his next attempt to improve conditions for his family. He decided that if he could find a small plot of ground somewhere on the outskirts of town where he could have a nice garden and raise chickens, maybe Johnny would be able to live there with the limitations of his disability. He could help by caring for the chickens and tending to the vegetable garden. Hopefully, Christina would be comforted if she could care for Johnny while guiding him in the garden and with the chickens. Maybe she would recall some of the pleasures of her childhood.

In a short time, he found a house on two-acres of property just outside of Collinsville, which was a small town on the bluffs about six miles east of Granite City. It was a two-bedroom brick home with a kitchen and extra bedroom in the basement. At the back of the property, there was a small orchard with four apple trees. The property was exactly what Traian had been looking for. He immediately had Pete make an offer on the Collinsville property and listed the Granite City property. Within two months, the transactions had been completed. Early in the summer of 1944, he and Bill moved in.

Now it was time to try to convince Teeny that it would be good for the two of them to be together again. On his next visit to Christina, he brought Bill to help with the persuasion. After dinner at a nearby family style restaurant, the three went back to Christina's apartment, where Bill showed his mother pictures of the house and grounds and explained how it would be good for Johnny to live there. Traian sat back and let Bill talk about the property and beg his mother to come home so that the family could be together again.

Christina sat silently and listened to Bill's pleas while concentrating on Traian's expression. She thought that their son seemed to be acting as his agent. Her feelings were similar to those she had experienced when Johanna had begged her to marry Traian. Again, she felt trapped.

Traian, for the most part, had his head down while his son was pleading. Occasionally, he would look up with eyes full of tears and see Christina staring at him. Christina saw clearly that she was needed, but was she loved? Showing no emotion, Christina agreed to come home, primarily because she saw that she was needed. Her relationship with Traian still needed to be sorted out.

Late in 1943, Traian was able to get Bill an appointment to Annapolis. Like his father, Traian had been contributing to the local federal congressional representative. He thought that an appointment to West Point or Annapolis would serve two good purposes. First, Bill would be able to avoid combat while attending one of the academies. Second, he would be getting a free education. Through his labor foreman, Traian was able to make contact with union leaders who also worked on his behalf.

The application forms for Annapolis were filled out and sent back with a transcript of the courses Bill had taken in high school along with his grades. The return mail from Annapolis was disappointing. Bill was not qualified to take the entrance exam that was required for admission because of the D grade that he had received in his second semester of trigonometry and of his taking no courses in chemistry while in high school. Through his union contact, the congressman's staff was contacted. After hearing of the problem, the congressman suggested that the appointee go to summer school and complete the required courses. Then the congressman would reappoint him in the fall.

Again, Traian sought help from Bucur. After helping Bill enroll in summer school at Washington University in St. Louis, he arranged for Bill to stay with Bucur's family while going to summer school, which was within walking distance. Bucur had purchased a new home on Oakland Avenue across from Forest Park. Living with him at that time were his wife, his daughter, and his aunt. His sons, Bill and Tommy, were in the service. Bill was in the army, and Tommy was in the merchant marines.

Bucur's family warmly accommodated Bill in typical Romanian fashion by providing him with the upstairs sunporch, which had been furnished with a daybed and a study desk, along with three meals a day with the family. Bucur made it clear to Bill that his studies came first. He would also be expected to help with chores around the house and at The Place when he was finished with his studies.

In the middle of the summer, Tommy came home on leave from the merchant marines. Bill listened with great interest to his accounts of sailing to ports in the Middle East while the German submarines were sinking allied merchant ships in great numbers. Tommy was in a program that was preparing him to be an officer in the merchant marines and brought home several large notebooks of classwork to be done while on leave. "These are far from complete," Tommy mentioned as Bill watched him set his notebooks on the bed during his unpacking.

During the general election in the fall of 1944, the congressman who had appointed Bill to Annapolis lost the election and the military-draft deferment that Bill had obtained pending his admittance to Annapolis was no longer valid.

Traian was very disappointed about Bill not being able to take advantage of the appointment to Annapolis. In hindsight, he recalled that during the last part of his senior year in high school, Bill had been applying less of his free time to studying at home and more of it on recreation. Traian began to feel guilty about enabling Bill's bad behavior. He hadn't given strong parental direction and had been too liberal by lending Bill the 1942 red Pontiac Club coupe for his social outings.

Early in December, Bill was drafted. He went by train to Chicago for his physical with a dozen other young boys from Granite City. After his physical, he came home and awaited the letter from the draft board for his induction.

On December 15, 1944, he boarded the train to Chicago from St. Louis's Union Station. Accompanying him to the station was Christina, who had tears in her eyes, and Traian, who was making every effort to keep a stiff upper lip.

Ioan had been corresponding with Traian from Romania about once a month. From 1930 to 1935, the letters were cheerful. Ioan was living comfortably with a few hired hands to help him on his small farm. After 1935, his letters became progressively less upbeat. He complained about the Romanian fascist party and the Nazi party's influence on the Romanian government. Nazi Germany needed Romanian oil.

Ioan, however, did take comfort from reading Nicolae Iorga periodicals, where Iorga condemned both the Nazi party and the Romanian fascist party as being harmful to Romania's best interests. In 1940, Iorga was assassinated by a Romanian-fascist death squad, and inflation was growing to the extent that Ioan's security was threatened. After 1940, Ioan's letters asked for food packages, which Traian and Christina prepared and shipped regularly at the beginning of each month.

Bill's overnight train trip ended at Fort Sheridan, an induction center a few miles north of Chicago. It was midmorning. He was issued his clothing, which consisted of two pairs of fatigues, a dress uniform, an overcoat, and underwear. He was also given a duffle bag to carry his clothes into the barracks where he changed and marched with his unit to the mess hall for lunch.

German prisoners of war were behind the counter dishing out food into the stamped-metal meal trays. Bill was told ahead of time by the cadreman in charge of his group that they would be served by German POWs who had been captured in North Africa the year before. During Bill's induction, the German army pushed the Allies back into Europe during their surprise attack, which was known as the Belgian Bulge.

The following morning after Bill's unit was awakened, the men were told that they would be working in the kitchen that day. The German prisoners of war were on strike, and the commander of Fort Sheridan had cut off the coal supply to their barracks as a means of breaking the strike. The outside temperature was near zero, and the strike had lasted two days.

From Fort Sheridan, Bill's unit rode in a Pullman car to Camp Hood, Texas. There he was assigned to an anti-tank company for basic training, which was scheduled to take five weeks. On his first assembly while standing at attention, Bill listened attentively to the barking of his first sergeant.

"Now you guys are going to fight an enemy, which has had twelve months of training along with combat experience. In five weeks, I am supposed to make you all into a company that will be a worthy opponent. I will be asking you to do things that you will not want to do. I know I can't make you do something you don't want to do, but I can make you sorry you didn't."

Bill took the comments seriously and found comfort in knowing that the corporals and sergeants who would be responsible for his training were a part of the American force that had invaded the Aleutian Islands, off the coast of Alaska, and had reclaimed them from the Japanese. He respected them for their combat experience.

While Bill was in basic training at Camp Hood, Traian was able to concentrate his attention on the rest of the family. Shortly after Christina came back, he arranged for Jane's return and enrolled her as a freshman at Collinsville High School. He and Christina visited Johnny regularly. Johnny was beginning to show signs of improvement from experimental medications that were becoming available for the treatment of mental illnesses.

On the way to one of their visits, Traian noticed a store that sold motorized, walk-behind cultivating equipment made expressly for small farms. After several visits to the store, Traian purchased the main piece of equipment along with the accessories he felt that he needed. This included a plow, cultivator, and grass-mowing deck. With these, he started his vegetable garden with Christina at his side.

Christina was having difficulty adjusting to her new environment. The neighborhood included a half dozen houses along their street. Each house was on a lot varying from one to two acres. The development had been made from a flower nursery, which was still partially in business and had its large greenhouse at the entrance to the subdivision. The subdivision was named Flora Place. Christina called it the wilderness. It was strikingly different from Granite City, where the houses were crowded together on small lots and she could have conversations with next-door neighbors through an open window or across a fence. Because her depression still lingered, she found it difficult to make new friends.

After several weeks of getting in shape with calisthenics and double-timing in ranks, Bill's training company was marched to an open place outside the containment area for a bayonet drill.

"Now pay attention, you knuckleheads," said his training cadreman. "This might save your life. When you and your enemy are out of ammunition, the only thing you have left will be hand-to-hand combat, and your bayonet could come in handy.

"If you approach an enemy with a bayonet, don't try to use your bayonet in a sword fight with him while he is still standing. Instead, approach him slowly and stare him in the eyes while keeping your bayonet pointing at his chest. Make sure you move to the right of his bayonet's point. Then as quickly as you can, push his rifle to the left—that's called parry left—rush forward, and give him a vertical stroke in his nuts with the butt of your rifle. While he is lying on the ground moaning, use your bayonet. Believe me, this is an effective move. It worked well for me in the Aleutians."

Bill watched the demonstration with uneasiness. He wondered if he would ever need to use a bayonet as he practiced this drill with a partner and an observing cadreman called attention to their mistakes in colorful language.

Early in 1945, Traian and Christina met with a young psychiatrist, who was Dr. Schwalb's assistant.

"There is a new oral medication I have been giving Johnny for the last month, and it appears to be working. The medication is still in the experimental stages, but Johnny's belligerent behavior has been considerably reduced. I think that we can let him go home and see how he reacts to the new living environment you have made available for him."

For Christina, it was like a dream come true. "That's wonderful. When can we bring him home?" she said with an excited look on her face.

"I don't want to give you false hope," the psychiatrist said turning toward Christina. "His trip home could very well be temporary, just like the medicine. There is so much we don't know, but I see no reason why we cannot arrange for a temporary release today. You can take him home with you."

Christina wept with joy while Traian sat quietly in deep thought. He was not emotionally prepared for the surprise.

Dear Mom and Dad,

Today we marched six miles to the rifle range. The range had about thirty targets in a line across a trench. A guy was assigned to lower the target into the trench after each shot. Then with a red disc about four inches in diameter, he would stick it over the bullet hole and raise the target so the shooter could see where the bullet went. If the shooter missed the target completely, the guy would raise the target and then swing a red flag across it. We called it Maggie's drawers, and everyone laughed.

My rifle is known as the M-1. It has thirty-caliber shells in a clip of eight. It also has a slight kick against my shoulder when I fire it. We fired at the target from three locations: 500 yards away while firing from a prone position, 250 yards away from a sitting position, and 100 yards away from a standing position. I was awarded a sharpshooter medal for my accuracy. It would have been an expert rifleman medal if I didn't have so much trouble holding my rifle steady while in the standing position.

I am really glad Johnny is home now. Please tell him hello.

Your loving son,

Bill

With Johnny now home, Christina's days were filled with enthusiasm as she found ways to keep Johnny busy helping her tend the garden and feed the little chicks in the brooder that Traian had set up in the basement.

Johnny was sleeping in the basement bedroom. Jane, who was now home and starting high school, had the spare bedroom upstairs. Traian built a simple A-frame chicken coop next to the orchard. Chickens from the brooder were placed in the coop after they had grown a little. At Christina's suggestion, Traian bought a small pig and placed it in a pen in the orchard.

Christina was more content now that Johnny was home. She also became more acclimated to her new environment, made friends with her neighbors, gave free haircuts, and looked after an older single woman named Katy, who lived in a small single-story house, which was three lots down the street. Christina made it a point to visit Katy several times a week with a hot meal and to make sure her immediate needs were being met.

Traian was also content. Things were working out with Johnny, who seemed to be calm because of the medicine. With two more years of high school needed, Johnny enrolled in Collinsville High School as a junior the same day Jane enrolled as a freshman.

Traian's day started at 7:00 a.m. when he arrived at the coke plant. His shift ended at 3:00 p.m. Traian was home by 4:00 p.m., after stopping for a beer at a tavern, which was halfway to his home. Before dinner, he made the rounds, checking the chickens, the pig, and the garden. Dinner was always one of his many favorite dishes prepared by Christina while Jane and Johnny did their homework. Because Bill was still in training at Camp Hood, he was not in active combat for the time being. Things seemed to be working out as planned.

The fourth week of training at Camp Hood was at a special location called Killer's College. Bill's battalion reached it by a twenty-mile march while carrying a full field pack, which contained a blanket, shelter half, trenching tool, mess kit, gas mask, rifle, and bayonet. During the march, the column of soldiers was occasionally sprayed with tear gas by a cadreman in a jeep. When the soldiers arrived at Killer's College, they paired off, combined their shelter halves, and set up their pup tents, which would be their sleeping accommodations for the next seven nights.

Killer's College used live ammunition to get the trainees accustomed to real combat conditions as much as possible. It started with the trainees squirming on their backs under barbed-wire entanglements, which the trainees held up with their rifles while live rounds from a thirty-caliber machine gun whizzed four feet above the ground.

Surprise targets were also arranged along a trail where the trainees walked with a cadreman, who raised the surprise targets with a trip wire. This required a quick firing response by the trainee. In the machine-gun-nest drill, a group of four trainees would walk along the trail. Suddenly, they would be fired on by a thirty-caliber machine gun with blanks. When that happened, three of the trainees would start firing at the nest from covered prone positions while one trainee would crawl around to the side of the nest and throw a dummy grenade into it from a prone position.

Grenade drill was a great cause for concern to the second lieutenant. His job was to lie next to a trainee who was supposed to throw a live grenade from a prone position. The second lieutenant had to throw the grenade if the trainee froze or dropped it after pulling the pin. Most officers got half-drunk before pulling that duty because of the danger that was involved.

The week after Killer's College, Bill contracted pneumonia and was in the hospital for thirty days. While in the hospital, Germany surrendered.

After being discharged from the hospital, Bill was assigned to cadre school. After a month, he was part of a team of cadremen who demonstrated how to fire fifty-seven-millimeter anti-tank guns to new trainees. During that time, Japan surrendered.

Bill signed up for a year in the regular army. He was assigned to Germany for occupation duty after a thirty-day furlough. Traian was glad to have Bill home for a month even though he spent much of his time borrowing the car right after dinner and partying in Granite City.

Early in 1946, Bill left for Europe on the *General Taylor*, a troop transport ship. He crossed the Atlantic on his way to Le Havre, France. From there, he went by forty-and-eight boxcars to Giesen, Germany, where troop assignments were made. Bill was assigned to guard duty along the border that separated the Russian and American zones of occupation. At that time, Germany was divided into four zones of occupation: the British, the French, the Russian, and the American.

Bill was assigned to L Company in the fifteenth regiment and third division. The company was billeted in a small hotel near the marketplace of Bad Köenigshofen, which was a small town about six miles from the border. Along the border, six sentries were assigned to four small villages, three days at a time. Sentry duty consisted of four-hour shifts in front of the guard's shack and road gate leading to the border.

"Now, here's your post, Bill," the sergeant said as Bill came to sentry duty for the first time. "About two hundred yards down the road, there is a squad of Russians with a roadblock. Farmers from the Russian zone with land in the American zone have passes to cross between the two zones. Farmers in the American zone with property in the Russian zone have a similar pass. Here is a sample copy of the pass that you will be checking."

"If there's a squad of Russians down the road, why don't we have a squad here?" asked Bill.

"The answer is simple, Bill. We bring a squad; they bring a platoon. We bring a platoon, they bring a company, and before you know it, we have two regiments facing each other ready to start World War III."

"Do they ever cause any trouble?" Bill asked with a look of concern.

"Once in a while, a couple of them will get drunk and fire some rounds this way to scare you. When that happens, don't fire back. Just get behind this big tree, and they will usually stop."

"But what if they don't?" Bill asked in a worried tone.

"Then ring me from the guard shack, and I will call Köenigshofen. They'll send out the riot squad to give you any backup you will need, if the Russians decide to come across the border and stir things up. So far, they've never done that, so I wouldn't worry."

More than half of the soldiers in L Company were combat veterans who had invaded southern France. They were waiting for their turn to be shipped back to America. Bill felt secure in their company and listened with great interest to their combat stories.

Between American outposts, the border was patrolled by former German soldiers, who were called border police. All of them spoke English and often stopped at the American outposts to bum cigarettes and chat with the American sentries. Bill always welcomed their visits and used them to learn German. After six months, he had mastered what the American soldiers called GI German. He had the vocabulary of a four-year-old German boy who swore a lot.

On one occasion, a border policeman and Bill got into a discussion about the existing political situation.

"There soon will be another war," said the border policeman. "It will be a war between the United States and Russia. This time Germany will fight alongside the United States."

"What about Romania?" asked Bill.

"Why do you ask?"

"My mother and father were born in Romania," Bill responded.

With that, the border policeman, with a faraway look in his eyes, said, "The Romanian soldiers that fought alongside us were fierce and brave but poorly equipped. Some didn't even have shoes and wore rags around their feet. But they will fight against Russia."

**L-Company, Mobile Constabulary
M-8 Armored Car, Mellrichstadt, Germany**

**Border Guard Shack Outpost 16
Emmelshausen, Germany**

Mellrichstadt, Germany

L-Company, Third Division, Koenigshofen, Germany
Bugler Sounding "To The Colors" Signaling the Arrival of the Colonel

CHAPTER 11
THE CONSERVATION YEARS

Early in 1946, Traian was promoted to superintendent of the by-products division of the coke plant. The promotion had both blessings and burdens. The blessings were not only an increase in salary but also bonuses based on the amount of coal tar, benzol, fertilizer, and manufactured gas that was produced. The manufactured gas was stored in a huge gas-storage tank. The tank had a moveable-domed top and telescoping sides. It not only stored the gas but also maintained a constant pressure on the gas inside it. This pressure was extended to the underground gas-distribution lines, which served gas ranges in the residences of Granite City.

The burden for Traian was keeping everything running. There were frequent shutdowns in the department due to defective valves and control devices, which had been left in place when the shutdown plant had suddenly started up to support the war effort. Many jerry-rigged repairs, which had been made to control devices and distribution lines, were constantly failing. Traian instructed those in charge to contact him immediately whenever there was a problem and he would come and assist in the repair. With Traian's technical knowledge and the hands-on skills of hourly workers, the problems were usually fixed within a few hours.

Occasionally, the process would have to be shut down temporarily, while waiting for a new part. This bothered Traian because the shutdown's amount of time reduced the quantity of material that was produced that month. To reduce the shutdown's amount of time, he started to spend his operating budget on critical replacement parts to have on hand, which eliminated the time he had to wait for parts to be shipped to him. Traian also established a friendly and personal relationship with the workers. They had a deep respect for him because of his openness while listening to their suggestions and complaints. To them, he was just Johnny.

"Johnny, I have a problem," said one of the workers.

"What is it?" Traian asked.

"It's about when I take my vacation. My wife thinks that I have been working here long enough that I should be able to take my vacation anytime I want instead of being told when I can have it."

"Well, you know that we can't let everyone select his vacation whenever he wants it because everyone would take it in the summer. We need enough people here throughout the year to keep the department running," Traian said. "But wait here while I go into my office and check on something."

After a few minutes, Traian returned. "I just checked with my wife, and she agrees with your wife. When do you want to take your vacation this year?"

The worker had a pleased yet puzzled look on his face before he was able to determine that Johnny's reference to his wife was a joke. He then countered with his own joke. "That's great, Johnny. Tell your wife she saved my marriage."

Dear Mom and Dad,

Good news! I was just promoted from private first class to buck sergeant. Why I was jumped over corporal, I don't know and didn't ask.

Our company was moved from Bad Köenigshofen to Mellrichstadt. It's a town about the same size, about five miles away. Our company is still going to the same small villages for border guard. I was told that headquarters moves each company about every three months to break up the black market connections between GIs and the Germans.

Also, all the combat veterans from L Company have gone home. Our company is no longer part of the third division but is now part of what they call the Mobile Constabulary. The company also has two armored cars. These are armored, rubber-tired vehicles with a thirty-seven-millimeter gun and a fifty-caliber machine gun. Why we need these, I don't know. I guess it is because the Russians are starting to move into the Middle East and the American headquarters' staff in Berlin thought the border should be better mobilized.

Anyway, it looks like Truman called their bluff, and the Russians have started withdrawing from the Middle East. My duty is now switchboard operator, where I maintain communications between the outposts and the riot squad.

I met our new company commander yesterday. He's a first lieutenant fresh over from the United States. I asked him if our company would be doing anything different since we are now part of the Mobile Constabulary. He said, "No. Just keep doing things the same way you have always done them in the past." So I guess there is nothing to worry about as far as the Russians are concerned.

Glad Johnny is doing well. Hope he gets to make new friends in high school. Will write more later,

Bill

Johnny's experience with high school seemed to go as well as expected. His overall mood was passive and somewhat shy. However, Christina and Traian were glad to learn that he had made a new friend, Nino, who was in his English class.

"Why don't you invite him over to visit us and have supper sometime? Dad could take him home," said Christina.

"What would we do?" asked Johnny, showing little interest in the idea.

"Well, you could show him the chicks in the brooder, the garden, and the pig. You don't know, Johnny. He might enjoy it."

Christina was right. When Johnny brought Nino home for dinner, the two of them seemed to bond well together as Johnny showed him around the property with a degree of enthusiasm that Christina had not seen for a long time.

Nino's interest was genuine. He was the middle son of a large Italian family. His father owned one of the largest grocery stores in Collinsville. Nino's father had started with a vegetable pushcart twenty-five years earlier. After graduation from high school, Nino entered the seminary and was ordained as a Catholic priest.

Just when everything seemed to be going their way, the medication Johnny was taking seemed to become less effective. His interest in life was diminishing. He was depressed and showed feelings of insecurity. After a week of these symptoms showing no signs of abating, Traian and Christina made an appointment with Dr. Schwalb so that Johnny could be reevaluated.

"It looks like his system is no longer reacting positively to the medication," Dr. Schwalb's young assistant said to Christina and Traian. "This has been happening to other patients with Johnny's problems. There are other medications that we can try. They are new and are still in the experimental stage. If you want, we can try them. But because of the uncertainty of his reaction, they should be given to him while he is hospitalized and under twenty-four-hour observation. Since you are in Illinois, I recommend that you have him committed to the state hospital in Alton. A psychiatrist there is a friend of mine. His work is going well with patients who are receiving these new medications."

Traian, saddened by the young doctor's diagnosis, sat motionless and stared at the floor. Although he was disappointed about Johnny's setback and was uncertain about his future, his main concern was for Christina. How would she react? Would this disappointment trigger another bout of depression?

To Traian's surprise, Christina accepted the inevitable. "John, honey, the doctor is doing all he can with what is known about Johnny's condition. The conditions at Alton are just as good as at Glenwood. The staff is friendly, and he will be close to home where we can visit him often."

Johnny's admittance to the state hospital at Alton ran smoothly. He calmly accepted his change in environment. In fact, he seemed to welcome the change, which gave Traian and Christina some comfort and peace of mind while on their way back to Collinsville from Alton.

Christina was resigned to the fact that she could do nothing to improve Johnny's medical condition. She could nurture his comfort by visiting more frequently with snacks and care packages. She joined a women's volunteer group that made regular visits to patients. She made friends with one of the members, Sophie Davis, who provided transportation for Christina's visits to Alton. Sophie and her husband had a business in Collinsville that sold secondhand furniture.

It was a little past midnight in Mellrichstadt, Germany. A phone call came from Emmelshausen, a small village near the American side of the Russian/American border, which separated the occupation troops from each country. The call was from the Emmelshausen squad leader to L Company's headquarters where Bill happened to be on duty manning the switchboard.

"L Company," Bill responded, after inserting the proper wire probe into the lighted port on the switchboard.

"Hey, Sarge. It looks like the Russkies are starting to have fun again."

"Yeah? What's going on?" Bill asked with little emotion since this kind of call had been coming to L Company's headquarters about once every two months.

"Not a whole lot. Just an occasional rifle shot toward our sentry."

"Is the sentry okay?" asked Bill. "How long has this been going on?"

"He's okay. Just scared shitless. He came back to the squad billet, and I sent him back with another guy to keep him company. It's been going on for about an hour. I think you might want to send out the riot squad, and hopefully, that will settle things down."

In routine fashion and as previously directed by his new company commander, Bill notified the new riot squad NCO, who happened to be in the motor pool playing cards. He sounded a little uncertain to Bill, after Bill had given him the information about the problems at the Emmelshausen post.

For Bill, it was a routine call for the riot squad. For the riot squad, it was anything but routine. All the combat veterans who had past riot-squad duty had been sent back to the States for discharge. Those that remained were green, inexperienced soldiers with a lot of vehicles, firepower, and enthusiasm. The only thing that they lacked was past experience and a commissioned officer to lead them.

Within a few minutes, everything in the motor pool that could move was headed for Emmelshausen. Bill watched the parade from a second-story window with a considerable amount of concern. Suddenly, the new company commander burst into the room, followed by his executive officer.

"Sergeant!" he screamed. "What in the hell did you do?"

"I did what I have always done in the past when the Russians acted up. I notified the riot squad."

"For Christ's sake, why didn't you notify me?"

"Well, sir, in the past, I never notified the company commander. He was always notified through the chain of command," Bill answered sheepishly.

The captain got on his walkie-talkie and tried to get ahold of his jeep driver, who was on his way to Emmelshausen, leading a convoy of two armored cars and four two-and-a-half-ton trucks. Each vehicle had eight green soldiers from the Mobile Constabulary but no commissioned officers. Never before had the Russian squad at the Emmelshausen border been met with such a show of force. Although leaderless, it must have been effective. No more sporadic firing was reported from the Russians by the American sentries.

For Traian, the summer of 1946 was for the most part good, except for his father, whose health was failing and whose financial situation was getting worse. Romania was now part of the Russian communist bloc. Living conditions for middle-class citizens had diminished to the point of bare subsistence. Letters from Ioan became less frequent and didn't mention the care packages that Traian had been sending.

In one of Bill's letters, he mentioned that passes were being given out to GIs in his company for weeklong visits to tourist points of interest in Europe such as Paris, Rome, and the Riviera. This gave Traian an idea.

———————●———————

Dear Bill,

I got your last letter about the riot-squad problem. I hope that by now, your company commander has gotten over being angry with you. Things are going fine here. Johnny has settled in pretty well at Alton. He seems to be accepting where he is. The new medication has calmed him down considerably. A new experimental brain operation is now being performed called a lobotomy, which the doctor has suggested we try. I am thinking it over.

Jane is doing well at school. She's very popular and seems to be enjoying herself. Your mother, as usual, stays busy all the time gardening, canning, cooking, and sewing. She also is involved with a women's group that goes to Alton Hospital regularly, visits patients, and helps them out with personal needs. She enjoys getting out every once in a while, and the companionship of the other ladies.

Bill, in your last letter, you mentioned passes being available for visits to other places in Europe. I wonder if you could get a pass to Romania and visit your grandfather? Just a thought.

It was good to hear from you. Write soon.

Love,

Dad

———————●———————

"Why in the world would you want to go to Romania?" the company's executive officer asked the young sergeant in the chair across from his desk.

"Well, I would like to visit my grandfather who lives in a small village near the border intersection of Romania, Hungary, and Yugoslavia."

"Your grandfather is Romanian?"

"Yes," answered Bill.

"Huh. I always thought you were Italian."

"Most people do, and I always thank them for the compliment," replied Bill, grinning.

After a brief smile of amusement resulting from Bill's self-deprecating remark, the chief executive officer gave Bill a serious look.

"There are a lot of problems with your trip. First, there will be a ton of paperwork with the Russians to even get permission for you to cross the borders of Hungary and Romania to get to your grandpa's village. And even if you were able to get the papers, you would be on your own, without any protection from people along the way—people who are so desperate that they would kill you just to get your shoes."

Traian was disappointed as he read Bill's letter that explained the problems with getting a pass to Romania. But he fully understood the dangers involved and accepted the fact that the only thing left for him to do was pray. He and Christina, throughout their married life, had been devout Catholics, had attended mass weekly, and had gone to confession often. Christina, however, still considered a four-leaf clover to be a sign of good luck. When she found one, she pressed it into her prayer book just to be on the safe side.

Traian was not superstitious. He believed that his body and mind were to be used for his own and his family's well-being. Like his father, he did not want to be a burden on his children in his old age. As far as his health was concerned, he was a firm believer in preventative medicine. Once a year, he went to Grant Medical Clinic in Clayton, Missouri, where he underwent a full day of medical examinations in order to determine and deal with any signs of potential medical problems.

Also in Clayton was his financial advisor, whom Traian visited twice a year to review his investments. The service that he received did include periodic statements of transactions, income, and value. However, Traian kept his own ledger of the same information to make sure no mistakes were being made. Traian actually enjoyed working on his ledger, which he looked upon as a hobby and proudly showed to Bill and Jane, saying, "This is something to keep my mind active and push back Alzheimer's."

Late in 1946, Bill was discharged from the army after a harrowing ocean voyage across the North Atlantic from Bremerhaven, Germany, to New Jersey. The ship was a Victory-class vessel, which was a smaller version of the Liberty ships that were built in large numbers by Kaiser Shipyard in California during the war.

Midway across the Atlantic, the troop ship was hit by a hurricane and steered its bow into twenty-foot-high waves. Bill, who was lying on the top bunk of a rack of four, felt the ship slowly rise to the crest of a wave, hover for a second, and then drop suddenly into the trough of the wave with a loud "whomp" that shook the entire vessel. This went on for six hours while Bill thought of the stories that he had read about Liberty ships breaking in half due to poor welding.

The following day was sunny and calm. Over the loud speaker, the captain assured everyone that the ship was okay. No structural damage had been done. He went on to say that in his thirty years at sea, this was the worst storm he had ever encountered. After the captain's remarks, the ship's chaplain offered a prayer of thanksgiving.

As the troop ship entered the Hudson River and the Statue of Liberty was visible to all on deck, Bill was contemplating what it would be like to be a civilian again, to be free to do anything that he wanted to do, and to have control of his life. Except for basic training and his bout with pneumonia, the last two years in the army had not been too bad. Now he was able to call his own shots. After his discharge procedures were completed at Camp Picket, Virginia, he boarded a train to St. Louis. The next day, he was home.

Traian, although glad to see his son, worried about his frittering away the opportunities that were now available to him, particularly the GI Bill. After a week of socializing with old friends, Bill was confronted by his father, who wanted to talk about the future.

"Well, son," Traian asked, "what are your plans?"

Bill said that he had been talking to an old buddy from Granite City who had just enrolled in the School of Architecture in Champaign, Illinois. "I was thinking of giving that a try," Bill said, showing a degree of maturity that Traian was not expecting.

Traian was both pleased and surprised with his son's response. "That sounds good. How much money from the GI Bill do you have for your education?"

"It looks like it will pay for eight semesters of tuition, books, and supplies and sixty-five dollars a month for living expenses while I am going to school," Bill answered.

"Do you think you can handle it?" asked Traian.

"I really don't know until I try. There is a University of Illinois extension college at Granite City High School. I thought I would sign up for four courses this fall and see how it works out."

Traian felt good about his son's answer but was still concerned about his study habits, which had not been good in the past. He had noticed a certain maturity in Bill's responses and had approached Bill's past study habits objectively in the conversation. In the discussion that followed, they both agreed that Bill could devote 100 percent of his time to classwork and study Monday through Friday and use the weekends for socializing. To facilitate this tactic, Bill would use his GI Bill money to rent a room at the Granite City YMCA. Traian would pick him up from the YMCA on Friday afternoons after work and return him to the YMCA on Monday morning.

With his concerns about Bill's future now somewhat in the background, Traian turned his attention back to Johnny. After further research on the possibility of the lobotomy, he found the procedure to be still very much in the experimental stage and decided against submitting Johnny to the operation.

"I just don't know," he said to Bill in the car late one Friday afternoon on their way from Granite City to Collinsville. "I am not worried about his surviving the operation. I worry about the operation making him a different person, maybe worse than he is now, or maybe some kind of vegetable with no feelings at all. I just can't do it."

———◆———

After two semesters at the University of Illinois extension in Granite City, Bill had completed his algebra requirements and several elective courses toward his degree. Traian was proud of his plan to have Bill study during the week and socialize on the weekends.

For the last five months, Bill had been steadily dating a Collinsville girl, Noreen, whom he brought home to visit now and then. Traian worried about the relationship becoming too serious and the possibility of marriage adversely affecting Bill's education. So far, things looked good, and Bill's grades were very high. He was temporarily relieved when Bill told him of his plans to go to summer school at the University of Illinois's extension college at Navy Pier in Chicago.

In early summer, Traian took Bill to Chicago, where Bill signed up for summer classes and found a place to stay at the North Avenue YMCA. When the summer courses were nearly completed, Noreen and her girlfriend Carol flew up to Chicago for a three-day-long visit. During their visit, Noreen and Bill decided to get married.

"Don't worry, Dad. I will still stay in school," Bill said to Traian, after he had told Traian and Christina about his decision to get married. "A lot of veteran students and their wives are living together on the campus, with their wives working full time. Nonie is an excellent secretary, and with my GI subsistence increased to $110 per month, we should be okay."

Traian was not worried about their financial situation. He was worried about their emotional strength to survive the difficulties and hardships of the sudden change that would occur in their lives and the pressures they were about to face. He was also worried about Johnny's medical problems being hereditary. Deep down, he didn't think it was, but he wasn't certain.

He wanted Bill and Noreen to have a consultation together with Dr. Schwalb, where he could evaluate their personalities along with their dreams and advise them accordingly on what they could expect in the changes and challenges they were about to face. Traian easily detected the pampering look Bill and Noreen gave him as they both reluctantly agreed with his request that they have a visit with Dr. Schwalb.

During their visit, Dr. Schwalb assured Bill and Noreen that Johnny's condition was not hereditary and spent most of the time telling them how hard the first two years of their married life would be. He focused on the fact that the difficulty would be greatest for Noreen, who would be away from home for the first time and alone much of the time because Bill would be spending most of his time studying.

"Architecture is a very time-consuming curriculum," he said in his concluding remarks. "But I think the two of you will be able to make it."

The wedding was set for June 26 of the following summer. An engagement party for the members of both families was held at Traian's house early in the fall of 1947. During the party, Bill, who was acting as bartender and was slightly over-serving, was pushing extra strong drinks on the guests to the embarrassment of Traian, who was talking with Bill's godfather, Bucur, while this was going on.

"Let me handle this," Bucur said to Traian. He went into the kitchen where Bill was mixing drinks. "Bill, you are mixing the drinks too strong. Carefully measure one shot for each drink. After the guest has finished his first drink and looks toward you, offer him a second. But never offer a third drink. Let them ask for the third."

Bucur's comments were made with a firm stare at Bill and a clear voice, which had a tone of authority. After that, Bucur left the kitchen while maintaining his authoritative look. He then rejoined Traian. Bill, who was embarrassed by Bucur's stern chastisement, followed his directions for the rest of the party.

The wedding... Late in 1947, major changes were being made by the state of Illinois mental-health department. With the increased success rate of new medications for mental patients, larger state hospitals began downsizing. Johnny was transferred to Galesburg, where the state hospital was developing a program in which hospital patients were selected to live in halfway houses and given simple paying jobs. Traian liked the idea even though the travel distance to Galesburg was over two hundred miles, which would reduce the number of visits the family could make to see Johnny.

Christina liked the idea. "It will be good for him to be in a halfway house with a job, John, and no longer in a mental hospital. I think that is as much as we can expect for now."

Traian was comforted by Christina's realistic and rational acceptance of Johnny's condition. He made it a point to visit Johnny once a month. He conferred with Jane and Bill before each visit so that they could come along and the family would be together for a few hours.

After a month in the Galesburg hospital, Johnny was transferred to a halfway house in Galesburg. It was a large residence in a middle-class neighborhood. There were eight occupants from the hospital and two caregivers. They found a job for Johnny. He worked as a busboy at a nearby restaurant. Along with the other occupants, he assisted with meal preparation and housecleaning. There were also group activities, including little dramas, which Johnny participated in with much enthusiasm.

Traian, now reasonably satisfied with Johnny's progress, began to turn his attention more toward other members of his family. Teeny, as far as he was concerned, seemed to be quite content. In spite of Johnny's move to Galesburg, she continued her volunteer work at Alton State Hospital, visited with neighbors, looked after Katy, tended the garden, canned vegetables, made jelly, and sewed her own clothes.

In a letter to Bill, who at the time, was living in an independent house on Sixth and Chalmers Streets in Champaign, Illinois, one block from the University of Illinois's campus, Traian mentioned, "Your mother is always doing something. Even when she is resting and watching television, she has a sewing project in her lap." Traian was glad that his son was moving forward with his education but was still concerned about Bill keeping up with his studies after he got married.

Jane was no problem. She was doing well in high school and seemed to be quite content. She was now a senior and was regularly dating a nice young man who was two years older and was an automobile mechanic. The gentleman's name was Don. Traian considered him to be mature and stable. Looking ahead, he thought that he might possibly be a good husband for Jane.

Don, who started taking flying lessons after high school, often rented a Piper Cub from a nearby airport on weekends. On such occasions, he would fly over Jane's house in Collinsville and dip the wings of his rented plane as a little hello signal to Jane. This always amused Traian, who by that time, was thinking that the relationship between Jane and Don was getting serious. Traian's thoughts were confirmed. Shortly after Jane graduated from high school, she and Don became engaged.

Traian was pleased. *It now looks like Jane's life is secure. She is going to have a nice husband, who I am sure, will be a good provider,* Traian thought, after Jane and Don had revealed their plans to get married on December 28, 1948.

Traian had a certain security regarding the marriage plans that his two children had made. The continuity of the family was important to him. He began thinking of the pleasures that would come from his grandchildren, and God willing, his great grandchildren. This began with Jane's first child, Karen, who was born in April 1950.

After Bill's first semester in Champaign, he came home early in June 1948. He and Noreen were married on June 26. Followed by a week's honeymoon in the Ozarks, Bill and Noreen lived with Noreen's parents during the summer while Bill worked as a laborer at the coke plant—a job that Traian arranged for him several weeks earlier.

Noreen continued to work at Gauen Lumber Company in Collinsville, where she was a favorite of the Gauens and all their employees. Fran Gauen had demonstrated this by paying for Noreen's and Carol's airfare to Chicago the previous summer and the rent for their Champaign apartment so that it could be held for the summer while Noreen had stayed in Collinsville to train her replacement. In addition, Fran Gauen wrote a very complimentary letter of recommendation for Noreen to Clarence Thompson, owner of Thompson Lumber Company in Champaign, which offered a job to Noreen the following fall.

Traian listened with great contentment as Bill told him his plans for the next fall while driving with him to the coke plant that summer. He was impressed with the generosity of Noreen's boss. Financially, he didn't need to be concerned for his kids. *Hopefully, it will get them off to a good start and take the edge off the problems they will face the first year,* Traian thought.

His hopes for Noreen and Bill were fulfilled. Bill graduated in February 1951 and was part of a graduating team that was selected by a large architectural firm in Detroit. This firm was producing drawings for the new General Motors technical center in Detroit. The project had been designed by the nationally known architect, Eero Saarinen, who had designed the St. Louis Arch. In January 1952, Noreen had her first child, Jan, in Detroit. The following fall, Bill was offered a job with a large architectural firm in St. Louis, and he moved his family back to Collinsville.

Traian was now content. Johnny was being taken care of as well as could be expected. Teeny seemed stimulating to him as their relationship and feelings for each other grew stronger. They enjoyed many common interests. To top it all off, his children and grandchildren lived close by where he could see them regularly. Finally, he could live securely and enjoy his life.

Johnny and Jane, 1945

Noreen, Bill, Jane, Anna, Christina, Eunice Wells

Christina and Johnny
1961

Traian's Pagoda and BBQ Pit

**Traian, Christina, Jane, Bill
1961**

CHAPTER 12
EARLY RETIREMENT

Early in 1950, Traian received a letter from Beba Veche, Romania. The envelope disturbed him. It was not from Ioan. He did not recognize the name or the return address. Traian's concern was verified as he read the letter, which had been written on behalf of his stepmother, Nanna Liana. His father had died. They had buried him in the cemetery next to the Romanian Orthodox church in Beba Veche. Although Traian had not maintained contact with his stepbrother, he felt obligated to call him and see what he could do to assist in Nanna Liana's welfare, now that Ioan had passed away.

At that time, Traian's stepbrother, John Crisan, was a prominent figure in the steamfitters' union, and Traian would occasionally come across his name in the newspaper.

"No, John, there is nothing you can do right now. We are maintaining contact with Momma and doing all we can to help her. I have contacted the Romanian embassy, and I am trying to bring her back to America."

Although saddened by his father's death, Traian took comfort in the fact that he was no longer suffering.

———————◆———————

From 1950 to 1955, Traian and Christina received grandchildren at a regular rate. Joining the Baby Boom generation was

Karen Sue, Jane's baby, born in 1950
Jan Marie, Noreen's baby, born in 1952
Michael Keith, Jane's baby, born in 1952
Donna Kim, Jane's baby, born in 1954
Kristine Ann, Noreen's baby, born in 1955
Donald, Jane's baby, born in 1955

Five of their six grandchildren were born in Collinsville. Jan Marie was born in Detroit.

Regular visits from their children and grandchildren gave Christina extra enjoyment. Jane was a stay-at-home mom. Her husband, Don, had earned the reputation of being an excellent mechanic—he was the leading one at the Cadillac dealership in Collinsville. With five toddling grandchildren, two in diapers, running around, and one of whom was usually sick, Christina spent much of her time babysitting her grandchildren. She had taught all of them to call her Baba, the Romanian term for grandma.

In early February 1956, Traian noticed an article in the *St. Louis Post-Dispatch* that told of an elderly Romanian woman who had been allowed to leave an iron-curtain country and to join her family in St. Louis. It was Nanna Liana.

At that time, countries behind the Iron Curtain were allowing older people who were indigent to leave the country. It made economic sense not to assist in their support, meager as it may have been.

The article mentioned that she had walked twenty miles to the train that had begun her trip to America. She had arrived in St. Louis without baggage. She had had a one-pound bag of paprika, which she had guarded.

Traian was in a quandary about what he should do to reunite himself with his stepmother. With Ioan's marriage to Nanna Liana early in 1924 and Traian's not seeing her for thirty-two years, he was wondering if reentering her and her family's lives would be an inconvenience for them, particularly since Ioan and Nanna's children had drifted apart after she had left for Romania. Traian decided not to intrude but to wait for a call from them, should his stepmother want to see him. The call never came.

"She probably is too old and sick to accommodate a reunion between our families at this late date," Traian said to Teeny.

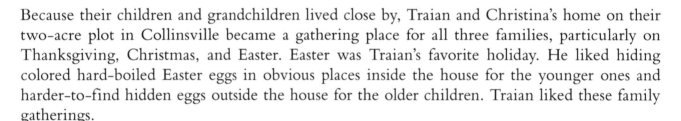

Because their children and grandchildren lived close by, Traian and Christina's home on their two-acre plot in Collinsville became a gathering place for all three families, particularly on Thanksgiving, Christmas, and Easter. Easter was Traian's favorite holiday. He liked hiding colored hard-boiled Easter eggs in obvious places inside the house for the younger ones and harder-to-find hidden eggs outside the house for the older children. Traian liked these family gatherings.

He had had a large brick barbecue pit built by two bricklayers that he had he hired from the coke plant. Soon after that, he had Bill draw up some plans of a screened enclosure for special events. For these events, he barbecued chicken and ribs over oak embers while Teeny prepared coleslaw and potato salad for those whom she called the tribe. As with the barbecue pit, Traian engaged two carpenters from the coke plant to build the enclosure.

In 1955, Noreen had her second child, Kristine Ann. She was named after her grandmother.

Traian began thinking about the future. On one of his visits to his financial adviser, Traian asked him to project an income for a retirement in 1966. Traian would then be sixty-five. For comparison, he had his adviser calculate an income for retiring in 1962, which was the earliest year that he would be allowed to draw social security.

"Factoring in your pension, social-security-health benefits, and income from investments, John, it doesn't look like there would be a whole lot of difference between the two," John's advisor told him. "In fact, if you retired in 1962, there would be enough cash in your portfolio for a down payment on a better home."

"Why would I want a better home?" Traian asked.

"I'm not suggesting you buy a new home. I am just letting you know that there will be enough money for a little luxury like a new car or something like that."

After their meeting, Traian began to think seriously about early retirement. The idea of extra time with the family and no more emergency calls from the coke plant in the middle of the night was appealing. Also, how long would God allow him to live?

Suppose I got run over by a truck right after I turned sixty-six. Then at least I would have had three happy, peaceful years behind me if I retired early. Thoughts like these raced through Traian's mind while driving back to Collinsville.

By the time he arrived home, Traian had made up his mind to retire early. However, he decided to keep the decision to himself as he began making preparations.

He was concerned about the coke plant. It had become part of his life. It was like a loud child with problems that needed perpetual care: hissing steam from the relief valves, constant operational problems, and a variety of chemical smells, which permeated his work clothes. It had a life of its own. Traian considered himself as its caregiver. He felt an obligation to leave the plant in the care of someone who was at least as capable as he was.

He had two younger assistants, either of whom would be a good candidate to take his place. He began spending more time with them, giving them his own thoughts on how to reduce the number of breakdowns and increase production. Not until the summer of 1961, did he tell anyone of his plans to retire.

By that time, Bill had decided to start his own business. He set up a one-man office in the spare bedroom of his house. Traian was not too concerned about his son's venture. "I think he has a good chance of succeeding. The economy is good now. If things don't turn out well for him, he can still find a good job in a large architectural firm. He is only thirty-seven years old," he told Christina.

Traian first told the blast furnace and bi-products division superintendent about his plans for early retirement.

"This comes as quite a surprise to me, Johnny. Are you having health problems?" asked the superintendent.

"No, it's just that I was beginning to get a little tired and thought it was time to let a younger kid take over before I got too old," Traian responded. He then told the superintendent about the two assistants and that he was grooming them.

"That's a good idea, Johnny, but don't say anything about your retirement plans to either of them until a few months before you retire. In fact, it would be easier for me if you didn't tell anyone until then." Traian gave his word that he would keep his plans confidential.

Late in 1961, Jane had her sixth child, Barbara Ann. Traian, who was happy to see the new addition to the family, began to worry about Jane's extra burden. He also began looking for a new location for Johnny. Johnny seemed to be doing quite well in the Galesburg halfway house, but the drive there took too much time, Because of all their children, it became more and more difficult for Jane and Bill to come along.

After searching for a nearby location, Traian found a shelter-care home in Alton, which would be a good place for Johnny to live. During Traian's visit to check the place out, he found it to be neat and clean with an adequate staff. It was a small facility, which accommodated twenty residents. It was owned and operated by a middle-aged woman.

Traian arranged for Johnny's placement in Burt Shelter Care Home soon after his inspection. By this time, Johnny's condition seemed to have improved slightly, but he still needed close monitoring with his medication. At Burt Shelter Care Home, Johnny could check himself out for short walks to get a milkshake or to attend mass at Saint Mathews Church, just a few blocks down the street. What Traian liked best about the whole idea was that now Johnny could be included in family gatherings on holidays.

Early in 1962, Traian began to finalize his early retirement plans by making it public. He told Christina first, who was surprised but not disappointed.

John has been working hard at the coke plant for the last twenty years. It would be good for him if he did not have to answer midnight breakdown calls anymore, she thought after he broke the news to her.

Then jokingly, she asked Traian if he knew what a wife's definition of retirement was.

"No," Traian responded with a smile. "What is it, Teeny?"

"Twice as much husband and half as much money," she said with a grin of her own while she stirred the chicken stew she had prepared for his supper.

"Well, that doesn't apply to us," Traian countered, this time with a serious look at Christina.

After dinner, Traian sat down with Christina. For the first time, she learned the details of their net worth from Traian's outline of the latest reports from their financial advisor and Traian's ledger.

In the past, as long as she could see how much was coming in and going out from their checking and savings account, which was slowly growing, she felt secure and didn't worry. Traian's fussing around with his ledger was a world apart from her. She looked upon it with little interest as a hobby of his.

Christina was surprised at the amount of their retirement income and sat quietly alongside Traian as he went over the outline of their living expenses after retirement, which was the same as they were presently spending with a 3 percent increase each year for inflation. One item caught her attention. It was titled "Trips." The amount was significant.

"What's this?" she asked Traian, pointing to the item without looking up.

"Well, honey, I really like to travel, and I think you do too. So I set aside as much money as I could for our enjoyment together, with a really nice trip once a year to anyplace we would like to go. I think I would like that more than a new car or a better house." Christina did not respond but looked at Traian with a pleasant smile, which he considered as her endorsement of his travel plans for their future.

There was one item, however, that Traian did not immediately share with Christina. That was his travel plans for the late summer and the early fall of 1964. He wanted their first trip to be as memorable as possible. Hopefully, it would be a trip around the world.

Over a period of several months, he went repeatedly to a travel agency. Traian was able to come up with an around-the-world package that he could afford. For this trip, he set aside a separate account for that purpose with a certificate of deposit through his financial advisor. The amount of the certificate was the cost of the around-the-world trip. The trip was to be Traian's surprise to Teeny at a time when he considered it was appropriate.

Traian then decided to tell the general superintendent of the coke plant that he had made a decision about which assistant he would recommend for his replacement.

"That's good, Johnny. I will see to it that he will be your replacement. Was there any reason that influenced your decision?"

"Well, I guess there were two," Traian answered. "First, he was a little older and had several more years of experience. Second and most importantly, whenever I got an emergency night call, I would call both of them and ask if they wanted to meet me at the plant and help resolve the problem. Sometimes one would come, sometimes both would come, and sometimes neither would come. But according to my records, Joe Hiles came most often, so that is who I am recommending."

"Great, Johnny. That's who it will be then. How do you plan to tell them?"

"Well, I was planning on telling only Joe tomorrow and recommending that he choose the other guy for his assistant. I do not plan to tell anyone else about my plans. The news will spread fast enough on its own," Traian answered and then left the office without any fanfare.

Now it was time for Teeny's surprise. After supper, while he was drying the dishes for Christina, Traian said, "Honey, there is something I want to talk to you about."

"Is something wrong?" Christina said while cleaning the sink. Traian seldom asked her to talk seriously about anything. Usually, something was worrying him.

"No, it's just that I have a surprise for you."

After supper while sitting next to each other at the dining room table, Traian showed Christina the brochures from the travel agency, which she slowly read with great interest without pausing or looking up at Traian. After reading them, she looked up at Traian and asked, "Why are you showing me these?"

"Would you like to go on a trip?" Traian asked.

"Well, yes," she responded. "But why are you teasing me with something you know we can't afford?"

"That's just it, honey. We can afford it." Then Traian showed Christina the certificate of deposit that he had squirreled away for the trip.

Christina sat there stunned. Her first reaction was anger toward Traian. What was a surprise to him was another scheme to coerce her into something that he wanted to do. *Why can't he trust me enough to be up front with me about his wishes rather than manipulate me,* she thought as the bad feelings from her rush to the altar threatened the joy that Traian was expecting her to have from his surprise.

But the past was quickly removed by her growing curiosity of the trip. She spent the rest of the evening going over the travel brochures with enlightened curiosity.

By the middle of 1963, Bill's architectural business was doing better than Traian had expected it would. He now had an office in Clayton with two partners and a good backlog of work. Traian had one less item to worry about while he and Christina began preparing for their trip with enthusiasm and excitement.

After Christina and Traian met with the travel agent to finalize arrangements for the trip, Christina reviewed the information regarding the limitations and recommendations for packing. The trip was scheduled for the fall of 1964. It involved leaving San Francisco on the luxury liner *Queen Elizabeth*, taking airline flights to eleven cities, and ending up in Rome. From Rome, they would take the *Queen Mary* to New York and fly back to St. Louis. The whole trip would take about five weeks.

With Jane's help, Christina began preparing the clothes she would take on the trip. After deciding what was needed and the baggage that was allowed, she went through her closet and identified what she had and then bought a few new outfits. She also selected patterns for garments that she still needed. These she sewed on the electric Singer sewing machine that Traian had bought for her shortly after she had moved into their house in Collinsville. The old treadle-operated Singer was now in the basement.

She enjoyed the flight from St. Louis to San Francisco where the tour began. It was her first time in an airplane. She sat next to the window where she could see the puffy clouds below and the Sierra Madre Mountains just before they landed. Traian allowed for an overnight stay in San Francisco.

The following afternoon, they met the tour group at the pier where the *Queen Elizabeth* was docked. They got up early and used their free time to visit Fisherman's Wharf before meeting with the tour group. Thirty people were in the group. Christina, with her outgoing personality, made friends with several women immediately. Traian engaged in brief but polite conversations with the husbands. The wives talked with the excitement as if they were long lost friends. Their stateroom, although small, was adequate, as far as Christina was concerned. Traian's mind flashed back to his accommodations on the *Carpathia*, when he had shared a much smaller space with three other women.

The five-day voyage across the Pacific ended in Honolulu. Christina spent most of her time with the friends she had made in San Francisco. Traian spent his time touring the ship and watching the waves. Again, it took him back to his voyage on the *Carpathia*. Both Christina and Traian looked forward to dinner, where they were able to meet new friends.

In Honolulu, they had a beautiful view of the circular swimming pool below their room. Christina, who always loved to swim, took a quick dip in the pool before their visit to the

Mormon Garden and their cruise to Pearl Harbor. That evening, their group met in the hotel lobby with their two tour guides and boarded a bus to the airport.

It was nine o'clock in the morning, Tokyo time, when they landed, after crossing four time zones and the international date line. It didn't take Traian too long to explain to Christina how they had immediately gone from Sunday to Monday after their plane had crossed the international date line and before it had made its fuel stop at Wake Island. Traian could see by her facial expression that she understood. She had given him the same look thirty-two years earlier, when he had helped her with the theory portions of her beauty course.

Their stop in Japan was one of the longer ones of the trip, allowing the group a full day to recover from the jet lag of the long flight from Honolulu. Christina decided to get Jane a gift. She purchased a nice set of china from a store near the hotel that the concierge had recommended. For Noreen, she bought a pearl necklace from a store that specialized in cultured pearls. It was at a tourist attraction that was located several miles from the hotel and on the coast. Customers could watch pearl divers retrieve the pearl-bearing oysters.

The remainder of their time in Tokyo was spent sightseeing. The summer Olympics in 1964 was held in Tokyo, and they were able to see the Olympic stadium with its huge sweeping curved roof, which was one of the permanent structures that had been built for the event. There also was the beautiful Chinzanzo Restaurant and Garden with its cascading waterfall. Traian took a picture of Christina in a soft light blue kimono, which she had bought for herself as a souvenir.

From Tokyo, they took a high-speed train to Kyoto, where they spent two nights. After Kyoto, there were side trips to see the fifty-three-foot-high bronze Buddha at Nara and the spectacular 330-foot Kegon Falls at Nikko. They also saw the five-story pagoda at the Tosho-gu Shrine. While in Kyoto, they visited Nijo Castle before arriving at the airport to board the plane that would take them to their next destination.

So far, the trip had exceeded their expectations. For the most part, Christina engaged in conversations with her friends and took in all the attractions. Traian acted as cameraman, making sure there would be a record of the enjoyment that he was sharing with Christina, who was prevalent in most of his photographs.

Their next stop was Hong Kong. After settling in at their Hong Kong Hilton room, they freshened up for dinner, which they had at the famous floating restaurant. While dining, they could see the Aberdeen Fishing Village (a large cluster of white-hulled, motor-powered boats that were partially covered with canvas awnings and in which the fisherman families lived). The boats were about twenty-five feet long. In the distance, they could see the older Chinese junks with their bamboo sails, which also served as homes for Chinese families.

The following day, they made a short trip to the border that separated Hong Kong from Red China. It was then known as the Bamboo Curtain. On their way to the airport, they stopped at Tiger Balm Garden, where Traian took Christina's picture with two young Chinese children, who were selling snacks to the tourists. After a forty-five-minute wait in the Hong Kong airport, they were off again to their next destination.

The flight took five hours. Their plane flew due south across the China Sea, skirting the eastern coast of Vietnam and landing in Singapore at the southern tip of the Malay Peninsula. It was a one-night stop. The brief stop allowed Christina to rest in the hotel most of the morning while Traian went on a walking-sightseeing tour with the group.

During the tour, he gave his camera to someone in his group and had his picture taken near a snake charmer, who was sitting between a large basket and its lid. The charmer was holding one of his king cobras. The other cobra sunned itself on the sidewalk, with its head at the edge of the curb. Traian kept a respectful distance from the snakes while the picture was being taken.

From Singapore, the plane flew north for three hours and landed in Bangkok, Thailand. This was one of the most memorable stops for Christina. Bangkok was the orient as she had imagined it to be—directly from the stories and the pictures in *National Geographic* magazines. They stayed there two days and three nights.

On their first day, their tour guide took them to the royal palace grounds, the Wot Ko Temple, the Temple of the Dawn, and the Pasteur Institute of Snakes, where the tourists went along a walkway where hooded king cobras sat six feet away, with no barrier between them and the tourists.

The second day was spent riding in the canals in two open power-driven boats, each having a tour guide. They were soon in the middle of the famous Bangkok floating markets. Dozens of small boats with fresh vegetables were being rowed to prospective customers by Thai women in wide-brimmed straw hats with flat tops.

A stop was made along the bank, where the group had a light lunch at a concession stand that was set up for tourists. Traian took a picture of Christina near a baby elephant. The elephant was being tended by a small Thai boy, who was being tipped for the photographs that were taken. Like Traian with the cobras, Christina kept a respectful distance from the baby elephant, which was resisting commands from its handler while the photograph was being taken.

The trip down the canal passed simple homes occupied by poor Thai families. The houses were built right up to the shoreline, where an open doorway with its sill over the water allowed Christina to see a mother bathing her small baby in a large pan. Christina was thankful for her abundant life in America as she said a small prayer for the young Thai mother and her baby. After the canal tour, the group boarded a chartered bus with their baggage and headed to the airport.

They were in the air for five hours, flying northwest along the western coast of Burma where it met the Bay of Bengal. Their destination, Calcutta, India, located at the top of the Bay of Bengal, was one of the most densely populated cities in India. India, at that time, was still struggling to establish its place in the modern world. The invasion by China in 1962, continuing problems with Pakistan over Kashmir, and the recent death of Prime Minister Nehru challenged the struggling economy of a nation that was trying to put on its best face to attract tourists. In spite of this effort, the teeming crowds of homeless poor could not be hidden from tourists. From the window of their hotel room, Traian and Christina could see crowds of begging poor people lining the sidewalks. Sick and dying people lay among them. For the most part, they were being ignored, except for the tender hands of Mother Teresa and her nuns.

The afternoon was spent touring a public park where sacred cows roamed freely. This was followed by dinner at the hotel.

By ten o'clock the next morning, they were on a short two-hour flight to Benares, which was a city along the Ganges River and a sacred location where thousands of pilgrims came to bathe. Christina, glad to be removed from the crowded streets of Calcutta, looked forward to the next special tourist event in Benares. This was a dinner at a private home. Traian and Christina's hostess was a middle-aged widow who lived in an upper middle-class home in the center of the city.

They were taken there by cab through a winding maze of narrow streets. Christina felt uneasy during this ride. She was worried about being separated from the rest of the group and was concerned about the cabdriver finding his way back to the hotel.

Her feelings of insecurity lessened with the welcoming greetings of their hostess, who was an attractive woman dressed in a sari that had been made from a soft-flowing material with several shades of red. She spoke English fluently. She had prepared a meal consisting of chicken, local vegetables, and a curry-flavored sauce. This was accompanied by flatbread and a spicy cake for dessert. Christina and her hostess found themselves heavily engaged in conversation, with Christina leading with questions about the life of her hostess.

From Benares, Christina and Traian found themselves on another two-hour flight to the city of Jaipur, where they rode an elephant to another tourist attraction called Amber Fort. Their last stop in India was the city of Agra, two hundred miles north of Jaipur.

Not far from this city was the most famous attraction of India. The Taj Mahal was their next destination. Christina, who had never had the opportunity to learn of the Taj Mahal during her grade-school geography or adult life, had no idea what to expect. However, she was filled with enthusiasm from the excitement being displayed by the other tourists as their bus carried them from the city of Agra to their final destination along a dusty road.

The day was hot. Christina was both impatient and uncomfortable. To make matters worse, there was a half-hour delay, which was caused by the bus having a flat tire. Finally, the bus came to a stop in front of a two-story, well-maintained building. Christina had a look of disappointment as she departed the bus. It really did not look that much different from the many other buildings she had seen so far.

Is this what we came all this way on a dusty road to see? she wondered. What she was looking at was the tourist's gatehouse to the Taj Mahal, which sold admission tickets to the famous tourist site and had a small souvenir shop along with public restrooms.

After leaving the gatehouse, Christina caught sight of the main attraction: a huge white marble structure at the end of a long narrow pool leading from the gatehouse. Christina found the dramatic site to be breathtaking. It was well worth the long dusty trip on the old bus.

As their plane left Agra, India, Traian leaned over to Christina, who was looking out the window at the cultured plains below.

"Well, honey, we are now on the other side of the world, halfway from home, and on our way back."

"It's really been a wonderful trip, John, but I'm starting to miss our kids," Christina replied pensively without turning her head. They had four more stops to make before hoarding the *Queen Mary* for New York: Jerusalem, Cairo, Istanbul, and Rome.

In Jerusalem, Traian took pictures of Christina at the Mount of Olives, with a view of Jerusalem in the background. He took another picture of her with a lady tourist friend in the Garden of Gethsemane. Memories of Egypt were recorded with pictures of Christina standing on a huge block of stone with the Sphinx and two pyramids silhouetted behind her against the sky.

Their short stay in Istanbul included a cruise on the Bosporus, the narrow waterway connecting the Mediterranean Sea to the Black Sea. Their final stop, Rome, was etched in their memories with the help of the pictures Traian took of Christina at the entrance to the catacombs, Saint Peters Square, Tivoli Gardens, and the Trevi Fountain.

Christina was exhausted by the time they boarded the *Queen Mary* and went straight to bed after their evening meal. Traian stood on deck and watched the dockworkers free the lines from the pier as the huge ship eased its way from the dock.

The next morning, shortly after they had steamed past Gibraltar into the Atlantic, Traian decided to go for a swim in the *Queen Mary*'s famous indoor swimming pool. It was early, and Traian had the pool all to himself. He eagerly dove into the water. The only problem was that he forgot to take off his wristwatch, which was not waterproof. Embarrassed by his own thoughtlessness, Traian sought peace of mind by confessing the incident to Christina. She seemed indifferent to the matter and remarked, "Well, John, it was an old watch, and you need a new one anyway."

As far as Christina was concerned, the remainder of the trip was uneventful. All she could think about was how much she missed her family. She couldn't wait to see them. At long last, they were picked up by Jane's husband, Don, at the St. Louis airport and were taken home, where the two exhausted travelers enjoyed a good night's sleep in their own bed.

View From Honolulu Hotel Room

Honolulu Hotel Pool

**Fujiya Hotel Garden
Niyanoshita, Japan**

**World's Largest Bronze Buddah
Nara, Japan**

**Kegon Waterfall
Nikko, Japan**

Buddhist Temple, Japan

**Floating Restaurant
Hong Kong**

**Fishing Village
Hong Kong**

**Tiger Balm Garden
Hong Kong**

**Stubborn Baby Elephant
Bangkok**

Canal Homes
Bangkok

Cobras, Pasteur Institute
Bangkok

**Snake Charmer
Singapore**

**Ride to Amber Fort
Jaipur, India**

Taj Mahal

Taj Mahal Gate House

Jerusalem, From The Mt. of Olives

Garden of Gethsemane
Jerusalem

**Sphinx and Pyramids
Cairo, Egypt**

**Cruise on the Bosphorus
Istanbul, Turkey**

Trevi Fountain
Rome, Italy

St. Peters Basilica
Vatican City

CHAPTER 13
THE GOLDEN YEARS

From 1980 to 1990, Traian and Christina experienced their golden years. They had good health and kept themselves busy. They worked together in their garden, with its rows of corn, potatoes, tomatoes, cucumbers, and peppers. By now, the chickens and pigs were gone, allowing Traian to cultivate nice lawns in the orchard and in the two adjacent vacant lots. Near the barbecue pit and screened-in pagoda, he put up a large birdhouse on a tall pole to attract martins.

Christina spent most of her time gardening, cooking, or canning. In the evening, she sat in the living room working on her knitting, crocheting, or quilting projects while watching television. Traian spent the day walking behind his Gravely tractor plowing, cultivating, or mowing the grass. Traian spent his evenings in his living-room lounge chair reading while Christina watched television.

Visits from their children and grandchildren were frequent. This happened during the day or in the evening. Christina welcomed the visits but did not stop what she was doing while she chatted with them during their visit. While Jane's youngest daughter, Beth, who was just out of high school, visited her grandmother, who was crocheting during the visit, she asked, "What are you making, Grandma?"

"I'm making a cover for the ugly old toaster," Christina said. "Even though it's old and ugly, it still works good. Is there something I can make for you?"

"Yeah. Crochet me a man who will make a nice husband," Beth said with a smile.

Traian missed the friendships that he had made at the coke plant. He joined a social group, which was called Glasgo. It was made up of existing and retired employees who met several times a year for an evening of steaks and beer at a clubhouse just outside Granite City. He often took his son Bill on these occasions. Seeing the popularity his father had earned with the existing and retired employees, Bill was proud of his father.

Trips were made regularly during the golden years. These included a driving trip to Alaska along the newly paved highway through Canada.

During one trip, while getting ready for bed at the Morwise Hotel in Whitehouse, Canada, they heard a loud commotion down the hall. A Native American, who had had too much to drink at the hotel bar, was causing a disturbance. Christina became very frightened, but she eventually calmed down after the guest was escorted to other accommodations by two members of the Royal Canadian Mounted Police. Traian took their picture as they passed by his door. This was added to other pictures: Christina standing in front of glaciers, totem poles, and forts. He developed and placed them in an album once they had returned to Collinsville.

There was also a trip to the Balkan countries of Romania, Bulgaria, and Yugoslavia. While in Romania, they stayed in the Hotel Intercontinental, a new twenty-five-story modern hotel with a gently curved facade and balconies. It was a dramatic contrast to the typical five-story buildings in downtown Bucharest. They were decorated with renaissance or baroque features. They faced wide, green parkways, which gave Bucharest the name the Paris of the Balkans.

From Bucharest, they went on a short day trip to the Castle of Vlad (Dracula), who was venerated by the Romanians for his resistance to the fourteenth-century invasion of the Turks. After they returned to Bucharest, they had an early dinner at a sidewalk café near their hotel. With them was their Romanian guide, Vasile, who was a medical student earning a little extra money as a tour guide during a brief vacation.

At that time, Romania was an iron-curtain country ruled by the Communist party and controlled by Russia. Its ties with Russia were being strained by the Romanian Communists who were making overtures to the west for tourists and trade. In spite of this, freedom of speech against the government was restricted, and the secret police kept their ears open to conversations in public that indicated resentment for the national government.

After a light meal with Vasile, Traian and Christina started speaking to him in Romanian to show their respect to him, as well as brush up on the language themselves, which they had not spoken in years. An older woman, who was seated at the table next to them, knew that they were tourists. She was surprised to hear them speaking Romanian.

Looking directly at Christina, she said, "Where did you learn to speak Romanian?"

"My family and my husband's family are from Banat. I came to America when I was young. But we still spoke Romanian at home while we learned English," Christina replied politely.

"But why would you want to come from a rich country like America to such a poor country like Romania? We have little to eat and empty shelves in all of our stores. The only people who have anything are the police and government officials, who are thieves." The old woman spoke loudly, making sure that the two middle-aged men sitting at the next table would hear everything she said.

Traian assumed that the two men were with the secret police and quietly asked Vasile for verification, this time in English.

"Don't worry," Vasile replied softly in English with his head turned away from the two men. "Yes, they probably are secret police, but they usually let old people blow off steam because they are not able to organize anything. But if I were saying that, I would be on my way to jail."

Before leaving for their room, Traian granted a favor that Vasile had requested. There was a severe shortage of consumer goods in Romania. However, there were shops in tourist hotels that sold items to tourists only. Romanian citizens were not allowed to make purchases from these stores. At the hotel's gift shop, Traian bought a pair of shoes, which were the color and the size that Vasile had given to him. The next morning when he met with Vasile for their day trip, they went into the men's room, where Vasile received the shoes and put them into his backpack.

Yearly, Traian went for his medical checkup and met with his financial advisor in Clayton. He continued to check the mailed copies of purchases and sales in his ledger. He also exercised regularly each morning, which included twenty-five push-ups.

Once, he tripped and fell down the basement stairs and broke his wrist. After a two-month recovery period, Bill asked, "How is your wrist, Dad?"

"As well as can be expected, I guess, but it still hurts a little. I can only do fifteen push-ups."

Traian always rode in the open VIP car, along with another World War I veteran, in the Memorial Day and Fourth of July parades. There was always a feature article in the local newspaper about him with his picture after the parade. Both Traian and Christina were active members of the Legion of Mary, which was a parish organization whereby husband and wife teams would make calls on former Catholics and encourage them to return to the church. Traian and Christina set aside several afternoons each month for this purpose.

Weekly visits were made to Burt Shelter Care Home, where Traian would sign Johnny out for an afternoon drive. Johnny's condition was stable. His medication kept him calm. During the afternoon drive, he sat in the back seat with either Jane or Bill and looked out the window at the farms as Traian drove along a country road. Johnny did not initiate any conversations but did respond to specific questions about his experiences at Burt Shelter Care Home, which were always good, positive, and short.

Pinochle games with Christina's brother Pete and his wife Irene were a regular occurrence. On one of their yearly trips, they drove to Yellowstone Park with Pete and Irene. There they stayed at Yellowstone Lodge while touring the park in Traian's car each day. Like their other trips, Traian recorded it with his camera, taking Christina's picture in front of Old Faithful and other points of interest in the park.

One evening in the fall of 1990, Jane came to visit Traian and Christina to get a few jars of canned pickles and applesauce, which Christina had made. Traian was sitting in the living room going over information that he had picked up for their next trip. It was a river trip on the Amazon through the rain forest. It was designed to bring the tourists close to nature with meals cooked along the riverbank and sleeping accommodations in tents pitched by the tour guides. Traian thought it would be exciting to be close to nature and to see natives living in the rain forest villages the same way that they had lived for the past several hundred years.

"Dad, you and Mom are too old for this kind of trip," Jane said while handing back the tourist packet she had just read to Traian.

"Why shouldn't we go? We're in good health, and I thought it would be something different for us," Traian replied. Christina sat listening while cross-stitching a quilt she had laid across her lap.

"That's not it, Dad. There's just too much that can go wrong on a trip like that. You would be out in the middle of nowhere. It would be hours or even days before you could get any help,"

Jane replied with a certain tone in her voice that Traian often heard when she was scolding her children.

"Well, there is another one that will take us through the larger cities of Chile and Peru with side trips to the ancient ruins of the Incas," Traian said, handing Jane a second travel brochure.

"Now, that's more like it," Jane said as she gave the second brochure a quick glance.

"Well, you're probably right. What do you think, Teeny?"

"Whatever you and Jane decide will be fine with me," Christina answered without looking up from her needlework. She never did like the idea of camping along a riverbank and had little interest in the native villages. Also, she was terrified of the thought of being close to crocodiles and anacondas while traveling the Amazon River in a small boat. Their trip to South America was their last big trip.

In 1993, Christina had a fall and broke her hip. She never completely recovered. She was confined to a wheelchair. Jane took charge and convinced her father that he was in no shape to care for Christina. After her operation, Christina was placed in a recovery center with the intent of later moving her into a nursing-care wing of the facility. This was an abrupt change in Christina's life. Having always been active and independent in the past, it took months for her to accept the fact that she would never go home again.

"Take me home," she would always say to Bill when he visited her.

"This is your home now, Mom," Bill would always respond.

"No, it's not. Take me to my real home."

Traian, while accepting Jane's advice concerning Teeny's care, missed her presence. Everywhere he looked, there was either something she had made or an item that had helped her make it. He visited her as often as he could and always came home with teary eyes.

Traian's frequent visits to Christina prevented him from visiting Johnny as much as he had in the past. He asked Bill to make sure Johnny was not forgotten while all these changes were taking place. After signing Johnny back in after a drive through the countryside, Bill stopped in to see the administrator/owner about Johnny's condition.

"Well, as you know, Johnny seems to be holding his own, but there is only so much we can do with his condition. He's getting older and soon may need the services of a skilled-care nursing home. There happens to be a nursing home in Smithton, Illinois, that has a wing devoted to people who have conditions like Johnny has."

Traian and Jane agreed that Johnny would be better off at Smithton, and Bill arranged for Johnny's admittance two weeks later.

Because Christina no longer lived at home, Traian found there was no longer any need for a garden. He told his brother-in-law Pete to have the orchard in the backyard and the two side lots divided into parcels and sold. After that was done, Traian found that he had a lot of extra time on his hands. He spent it driving to places that he was interested in.

One of these trips was to a gambling and casino boat in Alton. After his visit, he started to cross the street, heading for his parked car. It was early evening, and Traian failed to look both ways before stepping off the curb. He was struck by an oncoming car. The driver of the car happened to be the young fiancée of one of Jane's grandchildren. Having been to several family gatherings, the young girl recognized Traian, who was lying across the hood of her car, seriously injured, and unconscious. She followed the paramedics to the hospital's emergency room, where she called Jane.

"At his age, I don't know how he even survived the accident," the emergency room doctor told Jane and Don after Traian was stabilized. "He has several broken ribs, some internal injuries, and a lot of bruises."

Following a two-week stay in the Alton hospital, Jane arranged to have her father moved to Maryville Nursing Home and to become Christina's roommate. While they were roommates, Traian and Christina were the talk of the staff. It was common to see Traian pushing Christina in the wheelchair to the dining room and cutting her food. The movement of her arthritic fingers had begun to cause her problems.

They were always seen together holding hands, watching television in their bedroom, or with a group of residents enjoying an entertainment function. They both were happy and content and had frequent visits from their children and grandchildren. Soon great grandchildren began to visit.

Late in 1997, Christina's health problems became worse, and she was confined to her bed. Looking ahead and preparing for the worst, Jane discussed the situation with Traian and her brother Bill.

"I have talked with her about life support, and she said she doesn't want anything to prevent her from dying naturally," Jane said. "And she knows her time is near. I have made arrangements with the nursing home to get the papers ready for a signature. Dad, we are going to get Mom moved into a private room close to the nurse's station where she can be more conveniently cared for."

There was little response from Traian as he sat on the edge of Christina's bed while she lay there sleeping. "I guess that's the best we can do for her now," Traian then responded in a low voice while holding her hand.

Bill complimented Jane for the initiative that she had taken in addressing the problem. Having raised six children, Jane had developed a take-charge attitude when family problems arose.

"We all do what we can," Jane responded, grateful for the compliment. "I'll take care of Mom while you keep taking care of Johnny, and together we will work through our problems."

Christina's condition continued to deteriorate. She slept most of the time. On two occasions, she received the last sacraments from Father Quilligan, who was a close friend of the family's. Each time, she recovered consciousness. She was able to converse briefly with her children and grandchildren, who visited her regularly because they knew that her time was near.

On January 6, 1995, and shortly after receiving the last rites for the third time, Christina died peacefully in her sleep while Jane and Bill were present. Traian was in his room down the hall with his new roommate when Jane and Bill came in and broke the news.

"Mom has gone to heaven," Jane said as she stared tearfully at him and grabbed his hands.

Traian accepted the news without showing any emotion. For weeks, he had been expecting to hear the sad news at any time. On his regular visits to see her, he seldom found her awake. "Can I see her now?" he asked Jane, still not showing any emotion.

When they went to her room, Traian stared for a few seconds at Christina, who was lying in bed with a peaceful look on her face. With his eyes fixed on Christina's face, Traian walked slowly up to her, kissed her on the lips, and began to sob.

Jane took charge of the funeral arrangements. Traian had made the arrangements with Jane years before. He owned three lots in Oakwood Cemetery. In front of Johanna's and Persida's grave, there were plots for Traian, Christina, and Johnny.

The year after Christina died, Traian suddenly developed intestinal problems and was sent to Anderson Hospital for diagnostic tests. It was a severe case of colon cancer, which the doctor said had already spread rapidly. Immediate surgery was recommended.

The doctor had said, "I will know when I get in there and see what needs to be done, but right now, I must tell you frankly, things do not look good. Considering the size of the cancer and his age, if he survives the operation, he probably will not have muscular control over his bowels or urinary functions and will need to wear at least one and possibly two receptacle devices for the rest of his life."

Traian was wide-awake when he was given the news and told Jane, "Well, if that is all we can do for now, let's get the operation over with and see what happens."

Traian survived the operation and to everyone's surprise, did not need any receptacle devices. Following a quick recovery in the hospital, Traian returned to Maryville Manor. Although he was ten years younger, his roommate was confined to a wheelchair. This gave Traian a chance to feel needed. He took it upon himself to look after his roommate when assistance from nurses was not immediately available.

Late in 1999, Bill arranged a celebration for Traian's one-hundredth birthday at the neighborhood lodge. Traian enjoyed meeting family members, relatives, and friends, who attended in great numbers.

At the entrance to the lodge's driveway along the highway, Bill had a large sign made commemorating Traian's Romanian heritage along with his birthday. On the right side, there was the American flag. Under it was printed, "1909–1999." On the left side, there was a Romanian flag, under which was printed, "1899–1909." Between the two flags, "John Pistrui's 100th Birthday Celebration" was printed.

In the lodge, Bill had put up poster boards with pictures of Traian, from childhood to adulthood, including a map of Romania that showed the location of Beba Veche, where Traian had been born. There were also pictures of Traian with his coworkers at the coke plant.

After the celebration, Bill took him back to Maryville Manor. There the nurses had their own celebration.

Early in 2000, Johnny was also diagnosed with colon cancer. The doctor told Bill that the cancer was inoperable and gave Johnny about six months to live. Bill increased the frequency of his visits to Johnny, who soon became bedridden and for the most part, uncommunicative. Bill could tell that Johnny was aware of his presence by his widely opened eyes and the smile that Johnny gave him on each visit. The only communication was an occasional gesture that Johnny made. He would point to a picture of Jesus hanging on the wall at the left side of his bed. From these gestures, Bill sensed that Johnny was aware of his condition.

Bill had become acquainted with the hospice woman who had been assisting Johnny in his last days. One day, he received a call from her. She said, "Your brother is failing fast. I don't think it's going to be much longer."

Bill drove immediately to Smithton. As he entered the room, the woman from hospice said, "He seems to have recovered from his relapse. It doesn't look like he's ready to go yet."

Bill stayed for an hour, sitting next to Johnny's bed and holding his hand while Johnny stared at him with a peaceful look on his face. Then Johnny went to sleep, and Bill left. When he was halfway home, he got a call from the hospice lady. "Your brother just passed away in his sleep."

Bill was glad he was able to see Johnny before he had died. He immediately called Jane, who made the arrangements for Johnny's burial. The attendance at the graveside ceremony was small. It consisted of Jane, Don, Bill, Noreen, their children, and their grandchildren. Traian was also there. Bill gave a brief eulogy, recalling the memories of his childhood with Johnny before he became ill.

<hr />

For the next four years, Traian was in good health. He enjoyed regular visits from his family and the pampering of the staff at Maryville Manor. He still exercised each day, walking the halls once before lunch and once after dinner. He was alert and communicative, but he was eating less at each meal.

Early in 2004, his body began to shut down. He soon became bedridden. Jane began visiting him more regularly, making sure his needs were being properly met by the staff.

"I don't think he is going to last much longer," she told Bill after one of her visits.

On March 3, 2004, like Christina, he received the last rites. Jane notified the rest of the family, saying, "Dad's time is near. If you want to see him before he goes, you'd better come now."

One by one, Traian's senses and physical functions began to slowly shut down, just like the valves and control systems of the by-products division of the coke plant. Only in his case, there was no one there to repair or replace the parts to make his systems start functioning again.

The first thing to go was his ability to move his arms and legs. He could still see and hear. He recognized different family members who came to give their last respects. Soon he found it difficult to speak and gave up trying. However, he could still see and recognize members of his family as they came in. His sense of awareness was still keen.

He knew that he was not going to recover, but he was not ready to go yet. Then his grandchild Barb, Jane's sixth child, came in and paid her respects. "Hang in there, Grandpa. There is a great-grandchild on its way to see you."

Traian responded by winking an eye and attempting to smile. After hearing the news from Barb, who was the last member of his family to pay her respects, Traian, while still well aware of everyone's presence, began to relax. He was now ready to go. Gradually, the images of his family in the room began to fade, and soon he was no longer able to see. He could still hear and understand what they were saying. Gradually, the sounds of their voices began to fade out. Then he heard another voice … it was Teeny's.

**Traian and Christina
1980**

Totem Poles
Alaska

Fort Yukon
Alaska

Hotel at Whitehorse, Canada
Intoxicated, Peace-Disturbing Guest
Being Escorted To Other Accomodations

**Matanuska Glacier
Alaska**

**Portage Glacier
Alaska**

**Hotel Intercontinental
Bucharest**

**Hotel Intercontinental
Bucharest**

**Bill Pistrui and Sinzia Dragos
Romanian Embassy, London 2000**

Traian and Christina's gravestone, Lake Park Cemetery, St. Louis, Missouri

EPILOGUE

Traian is an example of millions of people who have immigrated to America since its founding. They were people with dreams. They were willing to take a risk by even coming here. They were also people with values, who put their families first and embraced the crosses that life placed on their shoulders, when they alone, were the only ones who could carry them.

Being the son of two parents born in Romania, I am proud of my heritage. I regret that I never learned the language as a child. My father tried a little too hard to shield me from being teased and to help me fit into a neighborhood where only English was spoken.

Nevertheless, I still feel the Romanian heritage, which was passed down to me by my parents, deep in my heart. I remember going to a Romanian Orthodox church as a child with my parents, the Romanian festivals in a St. Louis Park, where I played games with the children of other Romanian parents—children I didn't know—while our parents lined up and celebrated with Romanian folk dances (dances their parents did in the old country).

While doing some research for this book, I visited an Orthodox Romanian church service in St. Louis. After the service, I met with church members. The following week, I attended its annual Romanian festival. Saint Thomas Church brought back memories of the Romanian festivals that I had attended as a child.

There is no question in my mind that I am an American, but deep in my heart, I am also a Romanian. The heritage my father brought to this country is one that gave him the will and strength to care for his family when times were difficult and they needed him most. This kind of heritage, which embraces family values, exists today in the descendants of many immigrants, whether they are Romanian, Armenian, Bulgarian, Macedonian, Mexican, English, or Irish. They are all part of the melting pot that makes America great but are not the most important ingredient.

Sometimes we are too close to appreciate what makes our country great, and it takes someone outside our country to remind us. The following is a copy of an article written by a journalist in Romania shortly after the 9/11 World Trade Center tragedy and was given to me by my good friend Dave Wirz. Dave was a project manager at Korte Construction Company in Highland, Illinois, which is a design-build firm with major projects throughout the United States.

The firm was founded by Ralph Korte, a young man who was just off the farm, shortly after his service in the Korean War. Ralph was a hard-working example of Swiss-German heritage. He started by constructing farm buildings and ended up with a design-build construction company, which was doing over $100 million worth of construction when I worked for him. Ralph was a hands-on problem solver and a great leader. President Trump's effectiveness in problem-solving reminds me so much of Ralph, who although he has retired, keeps himself constantly busy helping organizations as well as individuals.

I happened to be head of the architectural division at that time. Dave and I interacted almost daily regarding projects that were under construction. Dave always teased me good-naturedly about my Romanian heritage. It was common to hear him say, "Give it to that little Romanian. Let him take care of it."

Here is the interoffice communication that Dave sent to all of us:

We rarely get a chance to see another country's editorial about the USA.

Read this excerpt from a Romanian newspaper. The article was written by Dr. Cornel Nistorescu and published under the title "C' Ntarea Americii" (meaning "Ode to America") in the Romanian newspaper *Evenimentulzilei* (*The Daily Event* or *News of the Day*).

An Ode to America

Why are Americans so united?

They would not resemble one another even if you painted them all one color! They speak all the languages of the world and form an astonishing mixture of civilizations and religious beliefs.

Still, the American tragedy turned three hundred million people into a hand put on a heart.

Nobody rushed to accuse the White House, the army, or the Secret Service that they are only a bunch of losers.

Nobody rushed to empty their bank accounts.

Nobody rushed out into the streets nearby to gape about.

Instead the Americans volunteered to donate blood and to give a helping hand.

After the first moments of panic, they raised their flag over the smoking ruins, putting on T-shirts, caps and ties in the colors of the national flag. They placed flags on buildings and cars as if in every place and on every car a government official or the President was passing.

On every occasion, they started singing "God Bless America!"

I watched the live broadcast and rerun after rerun for hours listening to the story of the guy who went down one hundred floors with a woman in a wheelchair without knowing who she was, or of the Californian hockey player who gave his life fighting with the terrorists and prevented the plane from hitting a target that could have killed other hundreds or thousands of people.

How on earth were they able to respond united as one human being? Imperceptibly, with every word and musical note, the memory of some turned into a modern myth of tragic heroes.

And with every phone call, millions and millions of dollars were put into a collection aimed at rewarding not a man or a family, but a spirit, which no money can buy.

What on earth can unite the Americans in such a way?

Their land? Their history? Their economic power? Money?

I tried for hours to find an answer, humming songs and murmuring phrases with the risk of sounding commonplace, I thought things over, I reached but one conclusion … Only freedom can work such miracles.

—Cornel Nistorescu

This deserves to be passed around the internet forever.

Looking at it as an architect, our freedom comes from the Bill of Rights, the first ten amendments of the Constitution, which was designed by our founding fathers. It is the foundation of our country. Family values and hard work from those who lived before us were the building blocks that formed the great nation we have today.

But unless a building is properly maintained like the by-products division of the coke plant, it will eventually shut down. To keep things running properly, we need thousands of committed, unselfish Traians as political leaders. We also need millions of vigilant helpers who select their Traians and assist in maintaining all the systems necessary to keep our plant running smoothly. It took a person on the outside looking in to see what we take for granted! *God bless America!*

ABOUT THE AUTHOR

My professional background started when I was selected as a member of a team from our graduating class to work on the architectural plans for the General Motors Technical Center in Detroit. The project was designed by Eero Saarinen.

Following that, I joined the St. Louis office of a large national architectural and engineering firm, working first as an engineer and then as an architect. This gave me the experience that was required to take the licensing exam for both professions.

After ten years with that firm, I started a one-man office in the converted bedroom of my home. This soon grew to be a respectable six-man office specializing in religious institutional projects. Fourteen years later, I merged my resources with Ralph Korte and assisted him in adding an architectural and engineering division to his fast-growing construction company.

In 1991, I retired. That lasted one month. Then out of boredom, I started a program-management consulting firm. After five years of leading the program-management company, I sold my interests to my partner and retired again. But the phone continued to ring. Local firms needed my temporary help. People needed my help with small projects.

So I am now back where I started: working on a drafting board in a small office, which was converted from a bedroom. Drawings are made manually on a drafting board with a straight edge and triangles because I was born thirty years too early to learn computerized drafting. I was in a management position when computerized drafting found its way into my profession. However, my line quality and lettering are still good. Also, I still am a good problem solver and am able to produce pleasing designs.

After my second retirement, I formed a small company to fill the needs of clients who were faced with complex design and construction issues that were outside the interests of the traditional architect/engineering firm. The firm was staffed with experienced professionals in the fields of construction management, architecture, and engineering. After five years, the firm grew to thirty employees before I sold my interest in Pistrui Consulting Group and retired again.

The following project profiles give examples of the problems we confronted, the way they were solved, and client feedback regarding the solutions.

Project:	High School Campus Expansion and Renovation
Client:	Granite City School District
Location:	Granite City, Illinois
Project Size:	$12,000,000
Project Scope:	This $12 million expansion and renovation to a bustling high school campus in Granite City, Illinois, included a 20,000 square foot addition for a state-of-the-art media center, library, and classrooms, plus a retrofit and completely new heating, ventilation, and air conditioning system for existing facilities—seven different structures built over a 70-year period.
Special Considerations:	As the project moved into construction, it rapidly became apparent that problems with the architectural drawings and other special issues would require numerous change orders to solve. Before long the project had a catalog of almost 100 unresolved RFIs (requests for information) on structural, electrical, mechanical and other issues. The school district ultimately terminated the design firm's contract, initiated litigation, and began to consider other resources.
	With the complex project in serious peril and with tremendous potential exposure, however, the school district found that other designers were reluctant to involve themselves. The risk was significant that the project would be stalled, if not completely halted. At this point, the school district sought out the Pistrui Group, which reviewed the situation and agreed to bring its program management skills on board on an emergency response basis to help tackle the problems.
Challenges:	Moving quickly to determine the extent of the problem, the Pistrui Group found other problems in addition to those already identified. These included major problems with mechanical and electrical system designs, improper capacities for conversion of a steam heating system to a hot water system, electrical feeders misplaced, an elevator mislocated, the removal of a number of bearing walls, a significant asbestos abatement problem not clearly identified, and many others. Meanwhile the project team itself was in disarray.
Solutions:	The Pistrui Group team took over management of the entire program. Immediately the Pistrui team set about performing due diligence on the myriad of RFIs, quickly identifying and correcting all omissions and deficiencies, and enlisting mechanical and electrical engineers to review and respond to errors in the engineering designs. It was quickly determined that a supplemental approach would not work, and that the drawings would need to be completely redone. Completion of new, accurate construction drawings was accomplished in phases, so that construction could proceed.

Using *PG*PM To Rescue a Crucial School District Construction Program

The project included a 20,000 square foot addition for a state-of-the-art media center, library, and classrooms.

PISTRUI
CONSULTING GROUP

A real challenge was the partnering effort needed for rigorous cost control and cost savings, and to get the program back on schedule.

Solutions: (cont'd)

In some cases, substantial redesign was required to correct problems or to cut costs. In one instance, to relocate an improperly placed elevator, a courtyard was turned into an atrium. At several points, redesigns by the Pistrui team eliminated the expense of removing bearing walls. In other cases, redesign eliminated future operational problems: reconfiguring light fixtures which would have been vulnerable to tampering and vandalism, and relocating a cafeteria area to isolate it from corridor traffic.

Another challenge was the special partnering effort needed for rigorous cost control and cost savings, and to get the program back on schedule in order to minimize disruptions to on-going operations of the school campus. To deal with these problems, the Pistrui Group team led a complete reorganization of the program. One of the measures adopted was the formation of a "vision team," including school and school district administrators, which could focus (in weekly meetings) on direction setting, mediating of conflicts, bridging of gaps between different interest groups, and making major decisions efficiently. Simultaneously, the Pistrui Group formed a program team to focus on the day-to-day problems and challenges involved in keeping the construction on schedule.

Results:

Within two months the program was essentially back on schedule, and within 12 months was actually ahead of schedule. Costs, which had threatened to soar as a result of the many layers of problems, had been brought back within available resource parameters. The quality, functionality, and usefulness of the facility had been ensured. And the frictions always associated with projects in trouble had been effectively mediated.

Comments:

"The Pistrui team came in at a very tough time and effectively took over things for us. They began correcting the plans and adding staff, and the project started moving again. Because most school superintendents will preside over only one or two capital projects in their entire careers, they don't have much of an opportunity to develop expertise in building programs. And cost containment is so primary. You need a program management resource who's familiar with school projects—a trouble-shooter who can pick up the pieces if and when things go wrong."

▪ **Steve Balen   Superintendent   Granite City Schools**

"When the problems were growing and multiplying, the Pistrui Group understood the magnitude of the situation immediately. They understood school needs. School renovations are much more complicated than new designs, so close proximity to your project site is imperative. Your designer needs to keep going to the site to see what the situation really is. The Pistrui team listened to our suggestions, encouraged us to present our ideas, and actively worked with us—even to the extent of plugging us into a basic computer-aided design program to provide our perspective on what solutions might work."

▪ **Tom Holloway   Assistant Superintendent   Granite City Schools**

Project:	New Residence Hall for 500 Students
Client:	Southern Illinois University-Edwardsville
Location:	Edwardsville, Illinois
Project Size:	$15,000,000
Project Scope:	Designed to provide badly needed housing for 500 university students, this new $15 million, four-story residence hall used pre-cast concrete construction technology for the building's central core and four wings. From the beginning of the project a key constraint which could not be significantly adjusted was the September move-in date for students. A parallel consideration was the need to modify the university center to provide the additional food service systems to serve the new students.
Special Considerations:	Based on a negotiated construction management approach with five prime contracts, the project lagged in getting the necessary initial approvals from the university's board of trustees. By January, the building was just getting out of the ground, and the project team was behind schedule while facing winter weather and an inflexible September deadline. Providing alternative housing at commercial rates would have been prohibitively expensive and complicated.

*PG*PM Gets a
New University
Residence Hall
Open Without
Slipping a Critical
September
Deadline

The SIU/Pistrui team integrated activities so that multiple project phases could be completed simultaneously.

As university officials became increasingly concerned about the schedule, their requests for assurance that project deadlines would be met received conflicting responses from the architect, engineers, the constructor, and the major subcontractors. At this point, the university asked the Pistrui Group to bring its management and technical expertise to the project team and develop approaches which would ensure that the project was successfully completed.

Challenges:	The Pistrui Group moved immediately to conduct a detailed analysis of the project's exact status, identifying specific problems and recommending solutions. In addition to being behind schedule, the project team was experiencing internal dissension, with growing disagreements between the architect and the subcontractors on how to address particular issues. No one on the team was available to effectively bridge the divisions between the areas of specialty expertise and represent the university's overall perspective. Issues with architectural drawings and specifications were requiring numerous change orders to correct. There were also difficulties with the mechanical and electrical systems and with the pre-cast concrete systems. There was no money in the budget for conventional project acceleration measures.
Solutions:	The Pistrui Group's analysis identified a number of project strengths to leverage (the subcontractor team was very capable, and so were the university's project coordinating functions), and laid out a strategy for addressing both the technical and schedule problems. The analysis determined that the project could still be completed on time if special measures were adopted immediately.

PISTRUI
CONSULTING GROUP

*The building's core and four wings
provide a distinctive, inviting residence
environment for 500 university students.*

Solutions: (cont'd) The strategy included team-building approaches to get the different elements of the program pulling together again, with the Pistrui Group providing positive leadership in frequent team meetings to bridge the gaps between specialty areas. It also included development of a new, detailed project schedule which phased the work for maximum efficiency, and carefully projected precise manhour needs at different points in the process. As part of its effort, the Pistrui Group developed a sophisticated project sequencing plan to accelerate progress on different floors and wings of the building to get the project team back on schedule.

To make up for lost time, the Pistrui Group's projections identified both the allocating of overtime work and the rechanneling of funding resources that would be needed to effectively accelerate the construction effort. In accordance with the new Pistrui Group project completion strategy, the university created an emergency fund which could accommodate special draws against the project budget as needed. Additional project management expertise was provided by the constructor.

Results: Almost immediately the project team was working effectively together instead of at cross purposes, and proved itself adept at handling subsequent challenges as they arose. The new flexibility in funding and scheduling permitted the team to swing the proper resources into play at exactly the right time and place in the construction sequence, and to integrate activities so that multiple project phases could be completed simultaneously. In September the project team was working late on the night before move-in day, but the bottom line was that the new residence hall was ready to receive the influx of students on schedule, and the project was delivered within acceptable budget parameters.

Comments: "The Pistrui Group did an outstanding job. They provided a real understanding of the educational environment, and without them we would not have been able to deliver the project on time. What the project team needed was someone who could view everything from the user's standpoint rather than from a specialized perspective. Along with everything else, the Pistrui Group became a team builder, gathered us together, and dissolved boundaries."

■ **Harvey Welch   Vice President for Administration   Southern Illinois University**

"There were times when I thought we would not make the deadline and would be over budget. The problems at times took a great deal of personal attention to iron out. But the Pistrui Group was able to provide exactly the special controls the project needed. They were able to focus effectively on details and to take a global perspective at the same time. They were a great project team to have on board."

■ **Michael Guerra   Construction Coordinator and Superintendent
Southern Illinois University-Edwardsville**

Project:	State-of-the-Art West Coast Distribution Center
Client:	Walgreen Company
Location:	Woodland, California
Project Size:	$65 Million
Project Scope:	This program required delivering a state-of-the-art 350,000 square foot automated distribution center (with nine miles of elevated conveyor systems) for one of the nation's leading retail and pharmaceutical marketers—on a tight schedule with an inflexible deadline for coming on-stream. To accommodate rapidly evolving market conditions, the scope of work for the complex project would need to grow and evolve even as the work went forward.
Special Considerations:	Because the fast track program would not have the luxury of a traditional planning phase, the Pistrui Group was brought on-board for its program management and project team leadership expertise early in the effort. Site selection was still proceeding and a preliminary project scope was still to be determined. Initial efforts included working with key internal functions at Walgreen (including logistics and distribution, architecture, construction, traffic, information technology, maintenance, loss prevention, and security) to develop lean project delivery approaches, then writing an RFP, reviewing and selecting the construction resources, and building a project team that could function smoothly under pressure.
Challenges:	The completion schedule was dictated by retail product cycles, with Christmas merchandise ordered more than a year ahead of time and set to arrive at the new distribution center beginning in June. The fast track schedule required the project team to make a number of critical decisions early, long before detailed program information was available. A key program management function, therefore, was identifying critical schedule and cost decision factors and getting project team attention focused on them early, weeks or months before the need was readily apparent.
Solutions:	As the project parameters began to come into focus, the Pistrui Group prepared design/build scope documents for a pre-engineered metal building with a 52-foot ceiling height and mezzanine spaces that could accommodate heavy loads and hanging conveyor systems. An engineering consulting firm was selected to provide mechanical and electrical scope documents. Benchmarks were established to hold down unit costs and change orders.
	In the selection of the project team, the Pistrui Group assisted Walgreen with interviews of four design/build teams and prepared a weighted point system for final evaluation. The design/build team selected included DES Architects/Engineers of Fremont, California, a full service architectural firm noted for its imaginative design capabilities and high quality construction documents.

Using *PG***PM** To Deliver an Automated Distribution Center On Time for Walgreen

Walgreen has used the new distribution center as a general prototype for similar facilities in other parts of the country.

Work was successfully phased throughout to accommodate installation of a complex system of automated conveying, sorting, picking, and transporting equipment.

The aesthetically distinctive, highly automated distribution center was completed on time and within acceptable budget parameters.

Solutions: (cont'd) The pre-engineered building structure would in fact need to be a specialized hybrid, using conventional metal skin and roof systems but going far beyond the manufacturer's capabilities in the structural engineering area. One unforeseen development was the special difficulties associated with meeting stringent structural requirements for the pre-engineered building due to its location in a high seismic area.

A key challenge was accommodating collateral, horizontal loadpaths for secondary elements of the structure (principally the conveying systems) with additional internal bracing. Because the building manufacturer, the conveying equipment provider, and the foundations structural engineering firm were not prepared to address the problem, the Pistrui Group identified, recruited, and worked closely with a specialist in seismic structural engineering to develop and implement solutions without seriously affecting the schedule.

Construction work was successfully phased throughout to accommodate simultaneous installation of a complex system of automated conveying, sorting, picking, and transporting equipment, with building systems and equipment systems tailored precisely to meet the needs of Walgreen operations. Configuration changes continued to be accommodated almost until the completion of the project.

Results: An aesthetically distinctive, highly automated distribution center was completed on time and within acceptable budget parameters. The new center performed well enough in fact that Walgreen has used it as a general prototype for similar facilities in other parts of the country. With continuing support from the Pistrui Group, major distribution center additions are planned in Mount Vernon, Illinois, Allentown, Pennsylvania, and Windsor, Wisconsin. The Woodland distribution center is the winner of an architectural design award from the state of California, demonstrating that design excellence and cost effectiveness are mutually achievable.

Comments: "On a program like this one, the dangers of allowing the design or the construction to stray from a strict focus can quickly place the entire project in unrecoverable jeopardy. A key skill is facilitating tight time schedules by offering reasonable, global solutions to design and engineering problems that demand early client attention. The Pistrui Group provides a valuable neutral perspective for complex projects, and helps the client team recognize when the schedule for addressing key elements of the project must be moved up."

■ Thomas Bergseth, AIA   Director, Facilities Planning and Design   Walgreen Company

"Finding and resolving the problem with the structural analyses for the seismic loadpaths is just one example of the Pistrui Group's effectiveness in building bridges between design professionals. In two other distributions center projects, the Pistrui Group was able to save Walgreen over $2 million by their direct involvement with our soils consultants and our conveyor engineers."

■ Dale Larsen   Manager of Construction and Maintenance   Walgreen Company

COMMENTS FROM THE AUTHOR'S FELLOW PROFESSIONALS

Bill Pistrui was and still is one of the most amazing individuals that I ever met in my fifty years in the construction industry. We first met when he was a partner in his own architectural firm on a project in Swansea, Illinois. There was a major issue that he reviewed, solved, and corrected with a minor cost to the owner and little shutdown time to the project.

He later joined Korte Construction and what a difference he made in design, consulting, and problem-solving. He never was arrogant or dominating at meetings and always looked for solutions that were beneficial to the subcontractors and owners, with little or no additional costs. He had an uncanny system of correcting issues that needed immediate solving.

I was in charge of the metal-building division at the time, and there seemed to be an issue with anchor bolts, manufacturer design, etc. on a weekly basis, if not daily, and Bill always had time to investigate and solve that problem with a smile while keeping the projects on schedule.

Bill always had a smile in the office and treated everyone with respect. I am proud to have been associated with him in the business and most of all as a friend. He was the best Romanian architect that I ever worked with.

Dave Wirz

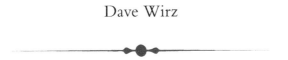

The first time I met Bill, I knew he was the right person to have in my corner. In fact, he quickly became the president of our architectural division and immediately went to work. His contributions have not only helped shape the Korte Company into the company it is today but have also helped redefine the design process for the construction industry.

A good architect knows how to create solutions through design. A great architect understands the importance of vision and ways to solve problems before they even arise. That was Bill.

Bill's upbeat and positive attitude as a coworker and as a friend is something I will always cherish.

Ralph Korte, Founder, The Korte Company

As an architect and divisional vice president of facilities planning, design, and engineering for the Walgreen Company, I had a career-long opportunity to not only work with hundreds of employees but also a myriad of consulting professionals throughout all the architectural and engineering professions. Simply put, the range of talent needed for our challenging and unyielding corporate goals were extensive.

The success of meeting constantly changing goals was entirely dependent on the synergy of the teams assembled to analyze and solve design and engineering problems, and as a result, the team member selection was probably the single most critical decision we faced.

I consider meeting and working with Bill Pistrui to be the best decision of my career as his collegial and intellectual approach to problem-solving became the center of our multiple successes in the design and construction of all of our large scale and complex projects. Bill's leadership and ability to bridge across professions was the key reason we constantly succeeded in our growth objectives.

I frequently think of Bill's crucial role in helping to provide a sense of dignity and respect in the process of developing the many critical and operationally important facilities we provide for our company. I am grateful for that.

I am not surprised by Bill's success as a writer at this stage of his career. It only serves to give clarity to his already extensive list of talents.

In addition, I wanted to say that the journey he celebrates in his book digs so beautifully at the heart of the immigration decisions our country and the world we face today. Nothing is more important than to celebrate our heritage and the wave of newly found freedom that courageous families like his found as they struggled to find their place in this new country.

How fortunate we are—for what we have, and for what Bill brings to each of us in his book.

Tom Bergseth

ACKNOWLEDGMENTS

I owe much to my immediate family, who became coaches and cheerleaders during the research, formation, and preparation of my original manuscript.

My oldest daughter, Jan Bowser, with her background in biotechnology and proofreading technical papers, kept me focused on my objectives.

My youngest daughter, Kristi Grabe, kept my spirits up as she read and praised the chapters that I gave her to review and guided me regarding the book's title and cover design.

Nonie, my devoted wife of seventy years, chose to be a stay-at-home mom after supporting me financially while working as a personal secretary to the president of Thompson Lumber Company in Champaign, Illinois, during my last two years at the University of Illinois. Nonie became my sounding board for the feelings and emotions that the women in my narrative experienced, as it developed, to make them believable to the reader.

With the support of my family, the research and preparation of the manuscript became an enjoyable experience that I looked forward to each day after routine and necessary daily tasks were completed.

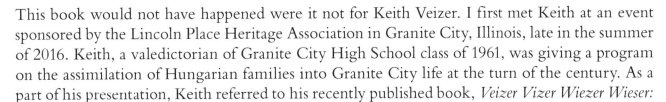

This book would not have happened were it not for Keith Veizer. I first met Keith at an event sponsored by the Lincoln Place Heritage Association in Granite City, Illinois, late in the summer of 2016. Keith, a valedictorian of Granite City High School class of 1961, was giving a program on the assimilation of Hungarian families into Granite City life at the turn of the century. As a part of his presentation, Keith referred to his recently published book, *Veizer Vizer Wiezer Wieser: A Memoir, Eight Stories, and a Search from Granite City to Kompolt.*

After the program I purchased his book, took it home, and started reading it. It was a page-turner for me, and I had a hard time putting it down before I completed it. Much of the book was about Keith's father, which inspired me to write about my father. As each chapter was completed, I mailed it to Keith, who corrected my grammar and punctuation while making suggestions for clarification. He was a great help to me in the process.

Keith, a former educator of English at the University of New Orleans, is now retired and living in New Orleans with his wife. He was a star tennis player in high school and is now deeply involved in the organization of national table tennis tournaments.

I also owe much to Bill Nunes, author of *The Big Book of St. Louis and Southern Illinois Crime*, from which I gathered historical information on the Cuckoo Gang, which was involved in the assimilation of my father's brother, Chiriac, into life in St. Louis in 1926. In my telephone call to Bill requesting permission to use some of the material of his book in my manuscript, not only did he give me permission but also offered to review my completed manuscript.

Bill, a speed-reader, read and edited my final manuscript in one evening. This was followed by a delightful evening at his home where I received copious comments on further refinements in grammar, punctuation, and historical accuracy. I was disappointed that he made no general comments regarding his opinion on the quality of my writing, but this was later gratified by the endorsement that he sent me after he received a copy of the final manuscript.

Bill is a retired social studies teacher from Collinsville Unit 10 District High School, where he was honored as teacher of the year in 1970. He has authored over seven books covering the history of southern Illinois.

I am also indebted to Cory Sever, the young artist who was inspired by pictures from the *Encyclopedia of Ellis Island* and *The Carpathia Book*. He placed my father and his family in selected pictures.

Cory Sever is based primarily in Illinois. He received his bachelor's degree in drawing from Milwaukee Institute of Art and Design. His focus ranges in a multitude of mediums, including painting, drawing, sculpture, and more.

I want to give a special thanks to my publisher iUniverse, which guided a first-time author through the many steps necessary in a successful publishing process. I am most grateful to Gil Maley, who kept me advised on the overall process regularly, and to Cynthia Wolfe in the editorial division, who helped me with the ego problem that occasionally led me in the wrong direction.

Finally, my deepest appreciation goes to Michelle Klees, a graphic designer with Minuteman Press. Michelle helped me with my original cover design and then became my contact with iUniverse through electronic mail throughout the publishing process. Michelle also patiently typed my line editing, which addressed the recommendations the editorial department offered on my original manuscript.

HISTORICAL RESEARCH

Family Genealogy

The family tree records of my father and mother, which date back to 1760, were prepared by my cousin Darrell Pestrue:

528 Pine Valley Road
Marietta, GA 30067
Email: dwpestrue@aol.com

Darrell's valuable research gave me the names of spouses and children, the dates of their births and deaths, and related cities. This information can be made available to interested readers who may feel they have a distant relationship to my father.

Missouri Historical Society

From this resource, I have obtained a block plat showing my father's first residence in St. Louis, utilities, and streetcar routes that were available in 1909. They were also very helpful in acquiring copies of the *St. Louis Post-Dispatch* regarding

- Queen Marie of Romania's visit to St. Louis in 1926,
- the rival gang shooting of a member of the Cuckoo Gang, and
- articles from the *Waterfront Journal* on the famous river-excursion boat, the *JS,* as it appeared in 1931.

World Book Encyclopedia

Maps of Romania's boundaries prior to and after World War I came from this resource. I also obtained Romanian political history that supplemented Nicolae Iorga's biography from this source.

"Chicago Skyride Photo." Amazon. Accessed December 19, 2019. https://www.amazon.com/Chicago-World-Original-Vintage-Postcard/dp/B00P5EUOTI.

"World Fair Maps." Chicagology. Accessed December 19, 2019. https://chicagology.com/century progress/1933fair42/.

"Entrance, Enchanded Island." CardCow.com. Accessed December 19, 2019. https://www.cardcow.com610215/entrance-enchanted-island-exposition-1933-chicago-world-fair/.

"Taj Mahal Photos." Google search. Google. Accessed December 19, 2019. https://www.google.com/search?q=taj+mahal&rlz=1C1EODB_enUS510US528&sxsrf=ACYBGNTMscfTmLV1wDAn7XNKqS6LgX4BTQ:1576694598116&source=lnms&tbm=isch&sa=X&ved=2ahUKEwjKncKL7b_mAhUQQ80KHRTVArgQ_AUoAXoECBEQAw&biw=1920&bih=920#imgrc=vXrIercITB6PFM:

Romanian Peasant Home photos were from a travel brochure.

BIBLIOGRAPHY

Nagy-Talavera, Nicholas M. *Nicolae Iorga: A Biography.* Isai, Romania: Center for Romanian Studies, 1996.

This book, a gift from Sinzia Dragos, was given to me at the Romanian embassy in London in 2000.

Nicolae Iorga was a Romanian professor, historian, and political activist, who was born in 1870. He was assassinated by a rival political group in 1940. He was a strong advocate for the unification of the Romanian-speaking provinces of Austria-Hungary into a united Romania. He fought for a better life for peasants in the periodicals that he self-published throughout his life.

Pickenpaugh, Roger. *Carpathia: A Biography of the Titanic's Rescue Ship.* Baltimore: Otter Bay Books, 2011.

This book covers in great detail the competition among ocean liners for European immigrant passengers to the United States and the restrictions for passage. The paragraph below, which is taken from page 28, is a good example:

> According to reports prepared by the American consulate, 2,816 would-be emigrants were rejected between the years 1910–1912. Most failed to pass the medical inspection to which all passengers had to submit. Conjunctivitis and trachoma diseases of the eyes were common causes for rejection … often the entire family would make it through the inspection process with the exception of one child … angry protests and attempts at bribery sometimes followed.

This happened to Traian's younger brother, Chiriac.

Moreno, Harry. *The Illustrated Encyclopedia of Ellis Island.* New York, NY: Fall River Press, 2010.

This book was of great value to me while writing the chapter on Ellis Island. The photographs of lines of immigrants undergoing the vetting process stimulated my imagination of what my father and his family could have undergone in 1909.

Nunes, Bill, Lonnie Tettaton, Dave Gruber, and Jim Cochran. *The Big Book of Southern Illinois Crime.* Self-published by the authors, 2010.

Chiriac (Uncle Charlie) often spoke of his personal encounters with members of the Cuckoo Gang at a local tavern in South St. Louis. Page 7 of Bill Nunes' book gives the Cuckoo Gang's history.

"There are dozens and dozens of books about immigrants and the hardships they faced as they escaped the woes of Eastern Europe, left relatives behind, and came to America as it beckoned to them with the Manifest Destiny promise of personal freedom and economic opportunity. Yet this one is a must read because it has a certain poignancy and truth that captures the essence of American ethos in action that is missing in most of the other immigrant stories. This tale will grab you by your lapels and hold you fast as you literally cheer and celebrate each success and root for the family to overcome various challenges. These intrepid people settle in Granite City, Illinois, one of those mid-sized towns located on the Mississippi River floodplain six miles north of St. Louis. Americans of all stripes and hue need to learn about places such as these because they helped form the industrial backbone of America that was responsible for democracy triumphing in two world wars.

The author does a masterful job of describing the flavor and ambience of his town as it readily accepted this influx of foreigners who would quickly assimilate, contribute, and become part of the great melting pot of America. It is a thoroughly enjoyable tour of the burg that would become known as the "Pittsburgh of the West," thanks to the steel and heavy industry located there. Strap on your seat belt and get ready for an interesting and fascinating read."

—**Bill Nunes**, *Author of Coming of Age in East St. Louis*

"Bill Pistrui's novel about the long and industrious life of a Romanian immigrant to America is based on a good deal of research, a patchwork of colorful and instructive stories kept alive in his family for more than a hundred years, and the experience of his family in America. Always in the background is the emerging manufacturing center, Granite City, Illinois – once called the "Little Pittsburg of the Midwest" – which was teeming with new arrivals from all over eastern and central Europe seeking prosperity and the freedom that comes with it. Like so many new Americans, the Pistrui's, father and son, made the most of their opportunities, especially educational opportunities, and excelled in their chosen professions."

—**Keith Veizer**, *Author*

CPSIA information can be obtained
at www.ICGtesting.com
Printed in the USA
BVHW022336121120
593075BV00004B/83